Eating Disorders

Eating disorders comprise a range of physical, psychological and behavioural features that often have an impact on social functioning and can invade most areas of the sufferer's life. Although eating and weight disorders are common in children and adolescents, there is a scarcity of practical guidance on treatment methods for eating disorders in young people.

In this book, Simon Gowers and Lynne Green bring together up-to-date research, clinical examples and useful tips to guide practitioners in working with young people, as well as helping families of children and adolescents to deal with their difficulties. *Eating Disorders* provides the clinician with an introduction about how CBT can be used to challenge beliefs about control, restraint, weight and shape, allowing young people to manage their eating disorder. Chapters cover:

- preparing for therapy
- a CBT treatment programme
- applications and challenges.

This practical text will be essential reading for mental health professionals, paediatric teams and those in primary care working with children and adolescents with eating disorders. It will benefit those working with both sufferers themselves and families who have difficulty understanding the disorder.

Online resources:
The appendices of this book provide worksheets that can be downloaded free of charge to purchasers of the print version. Please visit the website www.routledgementalhealth.com/cbt-with-children to find out more about this facility.

Simon G. Gowers is Professor of Adolescent Psychiatry at the University of Liverpool and Consultant to the Cheshire and Merseyside Eating Disorders Service for Adolescents. He recently led the NICE Guideline Development Group making evidence-based recommendations for the treatment of eating disorders in the UK.

Lynne Green is Principal Clinical Psychologist at the Cheshire and Merseyside Eating Disorders Service for Adolescents. She has clinical and research experience of treating both adults and children with eating disorders using the latest cognitive behavioural techniques.

CBT with Children, Adolescents and Families
Series editor: Paul Stallard

'The *CBT with Children, Adolescents and Families* series, edited by Professor Paul Stallard and written by a team of international experts, meets the growing need for evidence-based treatment manuals to address prevalent psychological problems in young people. These authoritative, yet practical books will be of interest to all professionals who work in the field of child and adolescent mental health.' – *Alan Carr, Professor of Clinical Psychology, University College Dublin, Ireland*

Cognitive behaviour therapy (CBT) is now the predominant treatment approach in both the NHS and private practice and is increasingly used by a range of mental health professionals.

The *CBT with Children, Adolescents and Families* series provides comprehensive, practical guidance for using CBT when dealing with a variety of common child and adolescent problems, as well as related family issues. The demand for therapy and counselling for children and adolescents is rapidly expanding, and early intervention in family and school settings is increasingly seen as effective and essential. In this series leading authorities in their respective fields provide detailed advice on methods of achieving this.

Each book in this series focuses on one particular problem and guides the professional from initial assessment through to techniques, common problems and future issues. Written especially for the clinician, each title includes summaries of key points, clinical examples and worksheets to use with children and young people.

Titles in this series:

Anxiety by Paul Stallard
Obsessive Compulsive Disorder edited by Polly Waite and Tim Williams
Depression by Chrissie Verduyn, Julia Rogers and Alison Wood
Eating Disorders by Simon G. Gowers and Lynne Green
Post Traumatic Stress Disorder by Patrick Smith, Sean Perrin,
    William Yule and David M. Clark

Eating Disorders

Cognitive Behaviour Therapy with Children and Young People

Simon G. Gowers and Lynne Green

Routledge
Taylor & Francis Group

LONDON AND NEW YORK

First published 2009
by Routledge
27 Church Road, Hove, East Sussex BN3 2FA

Simultaneously published in the USA and Canada
by Routledge
711 Third Avenue, New York, NY 10017

Routledge is an imprint of the Taylor & Francis Group, an informa business

Typeset in Times by
RefineCatch Ltd, Bungay, Suffolk
Paperback cover design by Andrew Ward

British Library Cataloguing in Publication Data
A catalogue record for this book is available from the British Library

Library of Congress Cataloging in Publication Data
Gowers, Simon G.
    Eating disorders : cognitive behaviour therapy with children and young people /
Simon G. Gowers and Lynne Green.
        p. cm.
    Includes bibliographical references and index.
    ISBN 978–0–415–44462–0 (hardback) – ISBN 978–0–415–44463–7 (pbk.)
1. Eating disorders in children. 2. Eating disorders in adolescence. 3. Cognitive
therapy for children. 4. Cognitive therapy for teenagers. I. Green, Lynne. II. Title.
    RJ506.E18G69 2009
    618.92′8526–dc22

                                                                            2008049341

ISBN: 978–0–415–44462–0 (hbk)
ISBN: 978–0–415–44463–7 (pbk)

Contents

Figures and Tables

Figures

Tables

Acknowledgements

The BMI/target weight calculator was prepared by Richard Janvier and based on original data from Cole Freeman and Preece (1995).

'Sam and Samantha' was conceived by Juliet Bartlett, Rachel Ellis and Caroline Bevan and illustrated by Imogen and Christy.

Figure 1.1 is reproduced with kind permission of the Royal College of Psychiatrists.

Figure 2.2 is reproduced with kind permission of Cambridge University Press.

Part I

Introduction

1

Eating disorders and their management

Introduction

Eating disorders are fascinating mental health problems in a number of respects. In the current climate of increasing concern about the growth in rates of obesity, they highlight the ambivalent attitudes to eating and weight which are shared by many people and the problems which can arise from them. However, although weight and shape concerns are extremely common, particularly in young females, full-syndrome eating disorders are quite unusual in children and adolescents, and rates of referral to secondary care services are rarer still. Despite this, anorexia nervosa (AN) has the highest mortality rate of any psychiatric disorder, and in the UK, it is currently the most prevalent disorder within inpatient child and adolescent mental health services (O'Herlihy *et al.*, 2003). In many respects, it is the paradoxical nature of eating disorders which makes them so interesting; this includes the typical love–hate relationship with food, young persons' investment in their disorder in the face of the physical and social disability it brings, and, consequently and crucially with respect to this book, young peoples' characteristically ambivalent attitudes to treatment.

Eating disorders are by no means new phenomena; medical reports of AN date back to the seventeenth century, and the Victorian physicians Gull and Lasegue both assembled enough patients to constitute sizeable case series. However, despite this lengthy history, the aetiology of eating disorders is complex and ill-understood, and, with the exception of adult bulimia nervosa (BN) (which was not described until the 1970s), there has been limited research into the development of effective treatments.

Classification

Concerns about children's eating and weight are extremely common. In young children, parents and other carers take responsibility for a child's eating, and feeding is seen as one of the core tasks of parenting. In the course of development (in keeping with other behaviours), children's own choices play a growing part, and control of eating gradually transfers to the young person. Responsibility for eating (and therefore to some extent for weight) is negotiated (though generally covertly) with parents in a similar way to other aspects of growing independence. The psychiatric classification systems (ICD-10 and DSM-IV) reflect this developmental shift in distinguishing between 'feeding disorders of childhood' and 'eating disorders', which generally develop in adolescence or young adulthood.

Feeding disorders arise in the first 6 years of life and involve food refusal or extreme selective eating in the presence of adequate food and the absence of organic disease. They are extremely common – faddy eating occurs in over 20 per cent of pre-school children; rumination and regurgitation of food more rarely. In contrast to adolescent eating disorders, there is usually an absence of concern with fatness or other psychological or behavioural abnormality, though difficulties can often be identified in the relationship between the child and the mother.

> Feeding disorders involve food refusal or selective eating

Eating disorders, however, comprise AN, bulimia nervosa (BN) and their variants. They typically develop in adolescence or early adulthood but sometimes arise in late childhood. The disorders share much the same psychopathology, and many patients migrate between the diagnoses or fulfil only partial syndromes. The ICD and DSM schemes for classifying and diagnosing eating disorders recognise the two main conditions, and their diagnostic criteria are similar. DSM-IV also lists a number of 'eating disorders not otherwise specified' (eating disorder NOS), including partial syndromes which are relatively common.

In practice, despite the above distinction there is some overlap between *feeding disorders* and *early-onset eating disorders*, i.e. those occurring in 8–12-year-olds. Eating disorders in this age group tend to be atypical and to confuse things further; such children often have a prior history of feeding difficulties. The terms 'selective eating', 'pervasive refusal' and 'food-avoidance emotional disorder' describe some of the atypical eating disorders of this age group.

> The main eating disorders are anorexia nervosa and bulimia nervosa

Anorexia nervosa (AN)

Four features need to be present to make a diagnosis of AN:

- Overevaluation of the importance of weight and shape; that is, judging self-worth largely, or even exclusively, in these terms. This is often expressed as an intense fear of becoming fat and sometimes referred to as a distortion of body image.
- The maintenance of an unduly low body weight (that is less than 85 per cent of that expected, or a body mass index (BMI) below the 2nd percentile for age).
- Active control of weight by dietary restriction, exercise, vomiting or purgation.
- A widespread endocrine disturbance involving the hypothalamic-pituitary-gonadal axis. This is manifest as amenorrhoea in post-pubertal females, pubertal delay in pubescent females and as impotence and lack of sexual interest in males.

Applying the strict diagnostic criteria for AN to the clinical problems seen in children and adolescents poses certain problems. For example, some common clinical presentations do not fit the adult-oriented diagnostic criteria. In this age group, a significant number of those who are underweight due to purposeful dietary restriction show little evidence of overconcern about shape or weight: rather, their dietary restriction appears to stem from the perceived importance of controlling eating per se. Strictly speaking, such patients should not be given the diagnosis of AN since a central diagnostic feature is not present. Of course, it can be problematic to identify this psychopathology in younger patients owing to the difficulty children have describing their thoughts, attitudes and behaviour, combined sometimes with a reluctance to do so. Obtaining supplementary information from parents and other informants is important and can be illuminating. The psychopathology of AN should, however, not be inferred without good evidence, and other diagnoses may have to be considered.

Another problem centres on the weight criterion of AN, since it is difficult to use with children and younger adolescents. There are two main reasons for this: first, adult body mass index (BMI) norms do not apply to younger age groups; second, growth may have been stunted, with a resulting risk of underestimating the degree to which a particular child is underweight. To address these problems, it is advisable to compare the patient's current percentile for age, gender, weight and height with earlier ones if possible.

The amenorrhoea criterion also poses problems in pre-menarcheal cases. Given the range of normal development, it can be difficult to estimate which girls might otherwise be expected to have completed their puberty if they had not engaged in disturbed eating and weight control.

> The key diagnostic features of anorexia nervosa are a distorted body image, extremely low body weight, significant dieting, exercise or purging, and endocrine disturbance

Bulimia nervosa (BN)

Three features are required to make a diagnosis of BN:

* overevaluation of the importance of shape and weight, as in AN
* the presence of recurrent binge eating, a 'binge' being an episode of eating during which an objectively large amount of food is eaten and there is a sense of loss of control
* the presence of extreme weight-controlling behaviour, such as strict dietary restriction, recurrent self-induced vomiting or marked laxative misuse.

The diagnosis of AN takes precedence over BN, and so the latter is a syndrome of normal weight.

It has recently been proposed that an additional eating disorder be recognised, namely 'binge eating disorder'. This is rather different in character from the other eating disorders and mainly affects middle-aged adults, so it is not particularly relevant to this book. A few overweight or obese adolescents will, however, regularly binge, with no compensatory weight-controlling behaviour, and thus fulfil this diagnosis.

> The key diagnostic features of bulimia nervosa are a distorted body image, binge eating, significant dieting, and vomiting or laxative misuse

Clinical features

The eating disorders are syndromes comprising a range of physical, psychological and behavioural features. They usually have an impact on social functioning and eventually their effects pervade most areas of the young person's life.

AN and BN, and most cases of eating disorder NOS, share a distinctive 'core psychopathology' that is essentially the same in females and males, adults and adolescents. Whereas most people judge themselves on the basis of their perceived performance in a variety of domains of life (such as the quality of their relationships with their family and friends, their work, their sporting achievements, etc.), those with AN or BN judge their self-worth largely, or even exclusively, in terms of their shape and weight and their ability to control them. This overevaluation of shape and weight results in a pursuit of weight loss and an intense fear of weight gain and fatness. It is important to note that it is weight loss that is sought, rather than a specific weight, so the subject never achieves a weight at which she can be content and relax her stance. Most of the other features of these disorders are secondary to this cognitive abnormality and its consequences (for example, dietary restriction and being severely underweight), and in Chapter 2 we will highlight the complex relationship between cognition, behaviour and physical features. In any case, in AN, there is a sustained and determined pursuit of weight loss and, to the extent that this pursuit is successful, this behaviour is seen as necessary rather than problematic. Indeed, successful dieting tends to be viewed as an accomplishment; as a consequence, young people with AN generally have a limited desire to change. In BN, equivalent attempts to restrict food intake are interspersed with repeated episodes of binge eating with the result that patients may see themselves as 'failed anorexics'. The great majority of these young people are distressed by their loss of control over eating, and this makes them easier to engage in treatment once they have presented to services, although because of associated shame and secrecy, they rarely do so on their own account before they reach adulthood.

The core features of AN and BN may be demonstrated in other ways. Many young people mislabel adverse physical and emotional states as 'feeling fat' and equate these with actually being fat. In addition, many repeatedly scrutinise aspects of their shape, focusing on parts that they dislike. This preoccupation may contribute to them overestimating their size. Others actively avoid seeing their bodies, assuming that they look fat and unattractive. Equivalent behaviour is seen with respect to weighing (weight checking), most patients weighing themselves frequently and as a result becoming preoccupied with trivial day-to-day fluctuations, whereas others actively avoid knowing their weight while nevertheless being highly concerned about it.

In AN, the pursuit of weight loss is successful, and a very low weight may be attained through severe and selective restriction of food intake, foods viewed as fattening being excluded. Anorexia (loss of appetite) is not usually a feature; rather, dietary control results in hunger, reinforcing fears of loss of control. Dietary restriction may also be an expression of other motives, including asceticism, perfectionism and competitiveness. Some young people engage in a driven type of exercising that also contributes to their weight loss. Self-induced vomiting and other forms of weight-control behaviour (such as the misuse of laxatives or diuretics) are practised by a subgroup who are more vulnerable to developing BN at a later date. Some have episodes of loss of control over eating, although the amount eaten is often not objectively large (subjective binge eating). Depressive and anxiety features, irritability, lability of mood, impaired concentration, loss of sexual interest and obsessional symptoms are frequently present. Typically, these features get worse as weight is lost and improve to a large extent with weight restoration. Interest in the outside world also declines as patients become underweight, with the result that most become socially withdrawn and isolated. This, too, tends to reverse with weight gain and provides a degree of reinforcing momentum to treatment. As body weight is maintained at least 15 per cent below that expected, pubertal development is stunted or reversed. This results in either a delay in the menarche or secondary amenorrhoea in those who have completed puberty.

The aim of young people with BN is generally to adopt the eating behaviours seen in AN. But unlike the very disciplined restricting anorexics, their attempts to restrict food intake are punctuated by repeated episodes of binge eating. The amount consumed in these binges varies but is typically between 1000 and 2000 kcals per episode, and their frequency ranges from once or twice a week (the diagnostic threshold) to many times a day. In most cases, each binge is followed by compensatory self-induced vomiting or laxative misuse, but a small subgroup do not 'purge', but control their weight with exercise or longer periods of abstinence. The weight of most of these young people is in the healthy range (giving a body mass index (BMI) between the 25th and 75th percentiles), as the undereating and overeating cancel each other out. As a result, patients with BN do not experience the secondary psychosocial and physical effects of maintaining a very low weight, though the disorder has its own adverse consequences. Depressive and anxiety symptoms are prominent in BN – and a number of patients engage in substance misuse and self-harm (particularly cutting).

Although both syndromes comprise a range of physical features, maladaptive eating behaviours and abnormal cognitions, in AN, it is the emaciation that is generally the most striking. A range of endocrine abnormalities result from calorie restriction and weight loss and affect most hormonal systems, though cessation of sex hormone production is usually the most evident in girls, as it results in amenorrhoea. Gastrointestinal features often follow the maladaptive eating behaviours. Dieting can reduce gastric capacity while bingeing, purging and vomiting (more common in BN) can have a negative impact on the whole gastrointestinal system from mouth and teeth onwards.

Origins of weight and shape concern

The aetiology of eating disorders is thought to be multi-determined, and the same is probably true of the belief in the importance of weight and shape that underlies these disorders. A genetic component probably plays a part in the aetiology of both eating disorders. However, this may exert its effect in a number of ways from predisposing to physical vulnerability factors (a propensity to obesity or early puberty) or to certain personality traits that also act as vulnerability factors, such as perfectionism or impulsivity. It has been proposed that a range of family, physical and personality variables might then lead to an overvaluing of the importance of weight or restraint, both of which can result in dieting behaviour. Dieting is generally an early feature of both AN and BN, both of which conditions can be seen as lying on a continuum of preoccupation with control (see Figure 1.1).

In classical restricting AN, the desire to exert control over eating and weight is often reflected in other aspects of the developing personality, the young person presenting as controlled, often obsessional and inflexible. The stereotypic young person with BN, however, shows alternating spells of impulsive loss of control with attempts at regaining it, often on a daily basis. This is sometimes also reflected in a more chaotic lifestyle, in which drug and alcohol use may be features.

It is the relationship between cognition, behaviour and physical features that has led to the cognitive-behavioural aetiological model, which will be reviewed in Chapter 2. This in turn provides the rationale for a cognitive behaviour therapy (CBT) approach. However, somewhat surprisingly, CBT has not yet been fully tested in clinical trials of adolescent eating disorders. We will therefore briefly review the range of other treatment approaches which have been proposed and the research evidence for their effectiveness.

Treatment approaches

The evidence for the effectiveness of treatments for child and adolescent eating disorders has been recently reviewed by the National Institute for Health and Clinical Excellence (NICE) in the UK, subsequently summarised by Gowers and Bryant-Waugh (2004). The NICE guideline made treatment recommendations classified from A (the strongest) to C (the weakest), depending on the strength of evidence. In considering the full range of psychological therapies, physical (including pharmacological) treat-

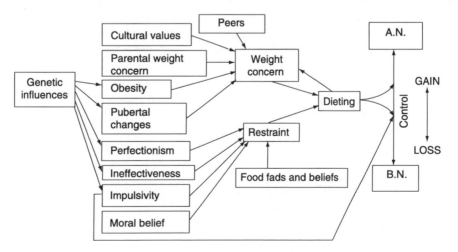

Figure 1.1 Origins of weight and shape concern (Gowers and Shore, 2001). Reproduced with permission from the Royal College of Psychiatrists. AN: anorexia nervosa; BN: bulimia nervosa

ment and service settings, the authors of the guideline were unable to make a single grade A treatment recommendation for AN across the age range, and the literature review revealed no randomised, controlled trials (RCTs) for BN in children and adolescents.

Guidelines on the management of child and adolescent eating disorders are therefore based mainly on expert clinical opinion and cohort studies rather than research trials. A number of academic bodies have published consensus guidelines, some specifically in relation to the management of children and adolescents. There is much greater emphasis in these on the management of AN than of BN, and on physical rather than other aspects of management.

> There is little robust empirical evidence to recommend any one treatment approach

Physical management

In AN, the guidelines refer to the potentially irreversible effects on physical growth and development, and argue that the threshold for medical intervention in adolescents should be lower than in adults. Of particular importance, is the potential for permanent growth retardation if the disorder occurs before fusion of the epiphyses, and impaired bone calcification and mass during the second decade of life, predisposing to osteoporosis and increased fracture risk later. These features emphasise the importance of immediate medical management and ongoing monitoring by physicians who understand normal adolescent growth and development.

Medical complications can occur in younger subjects before evidence of significant weight loss. In treating a malnourished young person, we should take care to avoid the refeeding syndrome, by regular monitoring. This is more common with parenteral than enteral feeding, and fewer problems arise in hospital when young people are eating normal food.

The Royal College of Psychiatrists recommends an energy intake in excess of 3000 kcal/day for weight gain, while the American Psychiatric Association (APA, 2000) suggests 70–100 kcal/kg body weight/day during weight gain and 40–60 kcal/kg per day during a weight-maintenance phase.

There is little in the NICE guidelines to direct the physical management of BN, though a key objective in planning dietary programmes is to break the vicious cycle of dieting and binge eating. Lethal medical complications are rare in BN, but trauma to the gastrointestinal tract, fluid and electrolyte imbalance, and renal dysfunction can occur. As in AN, attention to the adverse dental effects of vomiting and specific preventative guidance on oral hygiene is recommended.

Pharmacological treatment

The use of psychotropic medication is not considered a first-line treatment for eating disorders. A lack of studies and negative findings have led to the widely held view that the use of drugs is not justified in the first-line management of AN, and should be reserved for cases complicated by co-morbid diagnoses. With regard to depression, opinion is divided. Some hold that the depression that is commonly associated with low-weight AN tends to lift with restoration of physical health, and should be managed through psychotherapy accompanying weight gain. Others favour the use of selective serotonin reuptake inhibitors (SSRIs) even at low weight, although there is little evidence to support this practice. Clearly, in presentations complicated by a worsening of depressive symptoms, severe anxiety or obsessive-compulsive disorder, the use of medication can be considered. Tranquillisers or antihistamines are also often used symptomatically to reduce the high levels of anxiety in AN. Although there are no controlled studies, low doses of the atypical antipsychotics (particularly olanzapine) have been used to alleviate anxiety during refeeding. More RCTs have explored the effects of drugs in the management of BN than of AN. Guidelines have tended to conclude that although antidepressants of various types have been shown to reduce bulimic behaviours in the short term (by achieving reduction or cessation of bingeing and/or purging behaviours), there is inconclusive evidence about the persistence of these effects after the drug has been discontinued.

Ebeling *et al.* (2003) briefly reviewed the drug studies for BN and concluded that the use of medication as a primary treatment for bulimia nervosa in children cannot be justified due to the lack of evidence supporting it. However, taking into account the general reservations above, cautious extrapolation of research findings to older adolescents may justify the use of antidepressants as adjunctive treatments.

> Pharmacological interventions are not recommended for the first-line management of anorexia or bulimia nervosa

Psychological therapies

Although there are a considerable number of studies of psychological therapies in the recent eating disorder literature, a number of methodological issues make for difficulties in combining results in meta-analysis and reaching firm conclusions about the merits of different therapies. These include:

- heterogeneity within therapies of the same name
- the wide range of outcome measures used
- differences in timing of follow-up
- entry criteria
- other therapies given concurrently.

The NICE guideline concluded that there was limited evidence that a range of specific psychological treatments for AN with more therapeutic contact was superior to 'treatment as usual' (with a lower rate of contact) in terms of mean weight gain and the proportion of patients recovered. There was insufficient evidence from six small RCTs to suggest that any particular specialist psychotherapy (cognitive analytic therapy, CBT, interpersonal therapy, family therapy (FT), or focal psychodynamic therapy) was superior to others.

Family therapy

The psychosomatic conceptual model of Minuchin and colleagues stimulated considerable interest in the use of family interventions in AN, particularly in adolescents. Initially, the rationale was based on the notion of the 'anorexogenic family', but empirical study has failed to support the aetiological role of family dysfunction, and the model fuels concern about blaming parents. Family interventions have thus developed as treatments which mobilise family resources, whether delivered as 'conjoint' family therapy (FT), separated FT (in which parents and the child or adolescent patient are seen separately) or 'parental counselling'. There have been a number of RCTs, though the results are somewhat inconsistent. To date, several studies have compared different forms of family intervention in child and adolescent AN, but only two have compared FT with forms of individual therapy.

Russell *et al.* (1987), in a trial of patients whose weight had been restored in a specialist inpatient service prior to randomisation, found that for a small group ($n = 21$) of adolescents with short duration of illness, FT was superior to individual therapy. The findings in relation to those who had been ill for more than 3 years were inconclusive and the outcomes were generally poor. Robin *et al.* (1999) compared the effect of behavioural family systems therapy (BFST) with ego-oriented individual therapy (EOIT) in 37 adolescents with AN. Parents in the EOIT group received separate parental counselling. There was no significant difference between groups on weight gained or on psychological measures; however, the BFST group had a greater change in BMI over time, though this probably reflected different baseline values between groups. By 1-year follow-up, 94 per cent of the BFST group had resumed menstruation compared with 64 per cent of the EOIT group; however, 43 per cent of the series had also been hospitalised when their weight fell below 75 per cent.

Le Grange *et al.* (1992) and Eisler *et al.* (2000) compared conjoint FT with separated family therapy (SFT) in which patients were seen on their own and parents seen separately by the same therapist. The overall results were similar in the two trials, with a trend towards a superior outcome for the separated form of therapy. A small subgroup with high maternal expressed emotion did markedly better with SFT.

Studies of FT in BN have been more limited and so far inconclusive.

> Randomised, controlled trials of family interventions are limited and
> have produced inconsistent findings

Multiple family group therapy

The apparent effectiveness of family interventions with children and adolescents with AN and the need to develop more intensive, family-based interventions for those who require it, led to the development of multiple family group therapy. It aims to help family members learn by identifying with members of other families with the same condition, by analogy (Asen, 2002). It is generally delivered within a day hospital programme, in which up to 10 families with a child with AN, attend a mixture of whole family group discussions, parallel meetings of parents and adolescents, and creative activities. Preparation of lunch and communal eating is a central part of the programme. There is generally a 4–5-day block of therapy followed by a limited number of day attendances at approximately monthly intervals (Dare and Eisler, 2000, Scholz and Asen, 2001). This treatment is at an early stage of evaluation, but preliminary findings suggest a high degree of acceptability and promising outcomes particularly in terms of a reduced need for hospitalisation (Scholz and Asen, 2001).

> Multiple family group therapy is in the early stages of evaluation, but
> shows promise

Nutritional counselling

There is insufficient evidence to determine the efficacy of nutritional counselling given alone, though many services offer it as an adjunct to other specific therapies.

Dialectical behaviour therapy (DBT)

DBT is a behaviour therapy that views emotional dysregulation as the core problem in BN, with bingeing and purging viewed as attempts to control painful emotional states. DBT has been found to be more effective than a waiting list control in achieving abstinence from bingeing and purging in one small adult study (Safer *et al.*, 2001).

Cognitive analytic therapy (CAT)

CAT aims to combine cognitive elements into psychoanalytic methods, in a brief focal therapy. There are only two small adult studies of CAT in the eating disorders literature. In a small pilot study of those with AN (Treasure *et al.*, 1995), CAT was compared with educational behaviour therapy (EBT). CAT resulted in greater subjective improvement at 1 year and in objective outcomes on the composite Morgan–Russell scales, though these were not statistically significant. The Dare *et al.* (2001) study of four therapies, including CAT (see above), found no benefit of any one specific therapy over any others.

Motivational therapy and therapeutic engagement

There has been considerable recent interest in the importance of motivational interventions in the engagement and treatment of people with AN, based on the transtheoretical model of change of DiClimente and Prochaska (1998). Motivational interviewing is a potentially useful technique that aims to move people to a position where they are more prepared to contemplate change, and it is commonly incorporated into CBT programmes (see Chapter 4). These additions have yet to be evaluated fully in clinical trials.

Service issues

Most young people with AN, BN and related eating disorders can be managed on an outpatient basis, with inpatient care being only required for a minority with AN where there are serious complications related to co-morbid diagnoses, or where there is high physical and/or psychiatric risk (Nicholls and Bryant-Waugh, 2003). When admission is deemed necessary, this may be to a paediatric ward, a general child or adolescent psychiatric unit, or a specialist eating disorder service.

Anorexia nervosa

Research in the area of service provision is limited. There is one systematic review summarising what is known about the relative effectiveness of inpatient and outpatient care across the age range (Meads *et al.*, 2001). However, the review was based on only one small RCT with a 5-year follow-up, often referred to as the St George's study (Crisp *et al.*, 1991; Gowers *et al.*, 1994), and a number of very varied cohort series, making meaningful conclusions difficult. The main conclusions of the systematic review are that outpatient treatment for AN at a specialist tertiary referral eating disorder service was as effective as inpatient treatment in those not so severely ill as to warrant emergency intervention, and that outpatient care is in general cheaper than inpatient care.

Since then, a relatively large, multi-centre RCT of adolescent AN (the TOuCAN trial) has largely confirmed these findings (Byford *et al.*, 2007, Gowers *et al.*, 2007). A total of 167 young people were randomised to inpatient treatment; a specialist outpatient programme comprising CBT, parental counselling and dietary therapy; or treatment as usual in community Child and Adolescent Mental Health Services (CAMHS). Intention-to-treat analysis showed no differences between groups at 1- or 2-year follow-up, though full adherence to allocated treatment was poor. Those admitted to inpatient management after outpatient management had failed did especially poorly. The health economic analysis suggested that the specialist outpatient programme was the most cost-effective treatment (Byford *et al.*, 2007).

Specialised day patient treatment for AN has been described in the UK and abroad. A number of studies report short-term positive outcomes in older adolescents and adults. However, there are no RCTs, and it is not always clear whether, in the absence of the day care offered, the patients included in the study would have been treated as inpatients or outpatients. Although the addition of a day programme to a comprehensive service has been found to reduce the use of inpatient beds in an adult service, it seems unlikely that inpatient treatment will cease to be needed. The relative effectiveness and cost-effectiveness of the two forms of more intensive treatment have yet to be adequately studied.

It is widely believed that there are advantages in treating severe AN within a specialised tertiary eating disorders service compared with less specialised secondary services. Both competence and confidence tend to develop in settings where such treatment is a regular activity.

Bulimia nervosa

In the UK, very few young people with BN are treated on an inpatient basis. Admission tends to occur only in those with severe physical complications or with co-morbid presentations. It is generally recommended that the great majority of adolescents and adults with BN should be treated on an outpatient basis (NICE, 2004). The idea of 'stepped care' has been proposed for the management of BN, patients being offered simpler and less expensive interventions first, with more complex and expensive interventions reserved for those who have not benefited.

The place of inpatient treatment for BN is not clearly supported by research evidence. There are some reports of specialist treatment programmes for severe BN complicated by self-harm, substance abuse and suicidality in patients who commonly fulfil criteria for borderline personality disorder, but there are no studies investigating these issues in adolescents.

Prognosis and outcome

The course of an eating disorder is extremely variable and may range from a brief, mild episode leading to full recovery, to an illness with a chronic course lasting many years and sometimes resulting in a fatal outcome. In childhood and adolescence, this variability is especially marked, and without the benefit of hindsight it can be difficult to predict how the condition will develop in a given young person.

In thinking about outcomes and prognosis, there are a number of ways in which young people are different from adults, chiefly because they are at a different developmental stage. In adult-onset AN, recovery generally implies restoration to a premorbid state of physical health; that is, return of weight and hormonal functioning against a background of completed growth. In pubescent girls, treatment-imposed weight gain may precipitate growth and the menarche, with all the attendant physical and social implications. A recovering adult might anticipate return to a previous level of social functioning and occupation, whereas a young person's recovery will mean climbing back onto a normal developmental path. In short, a positive outcome for a child or adolescent involves facing a degree of uncertainty around physical and social identity that has not been experienced before. In a number of respects, this will mean 'growing up', and facing the anxieties that may have played a part in the original development of the condition. A related issue concerns the need to ensure that the 'recovered' child or adolescent continues to make developmental progress in the ensuing months or years. That is to say, a 13-year-old restored to a normal weight might be considered recovered *to date*, but the child's health will decline if he is unable to keep pace with the 'moving goalposts' of normal physical and social development.

Making clear statements about outcomes is difficult, because of a number of shortcomings in many of the published treatment trials.

Anorexia nervosa

General outcomes are often reported as good, intermediate/fair, or poor, with good outcome generally equating to full recovery.

A systematic review of 119 outcome studies of AN ($n = 5590$ subjects), found good outcome in 46.9 per cent, intermediate outcome in 33.5 per cent and poor outcome in 20.8 per cent. There was a trend towards a better outcome in younger patients (below 17 years at onset) (Steinhausen, 2002).

Rates of recovery usually increase with a longer duration of follow-up. The number of adolescent-onset cases recovering, increased from 46 per cent of those followed up for less than 4 years to 76 per cent of those followed up for longer than 10 years. In one series (Strober *et al.*, 1997), mean time to recovery ranged between 57 and 79 months, and full recovery was uncommon in the first 3 years. However, relapse after full recovery was uncommon. It should be noted, though, that most studies have found an increase in reported deaths with increasing length of follow-up. Although adolescent-onset series report better outcomes than adult-onset series, the very young (particularly prepubertal cases) appear to have poor outcomes. There is no conclusive evidence that gender or socio-economic status has a significant effect on outcome of AN. Various psychological symptoms associated with AN have been reported to affect outcome, and a shorter duration of symptoms at presentation seems favourable. The bulimic subtype, that is, vomiting, bulimia and purgative abuse, has been consistently found to predict a poor outcome, as has excessive exercise.

Outcome is often reported as less favourable in the presence of other psychiatric disorders, suicidal behaviour, personality disorder or substance abuse. Co-morbid mood disorders are well documented, but the relationship between these and outcome is unclear.

Poor childhood social adjustment predicts a poor outcome, as does disturbed relationships with or between parents. Conversely, a good parent–child relationship appears to be associated with a favourable outcome. An interview-based study found that poor family functioning, as rated by either a clinician or the young person themselves, predicted a poor outcome at 1 and 2 years, while the parent's assessment of the family's functioning had no predictive power (North *et al.*, 1997).

Mortality

The majority of outcome studies on AN report crude mortality rates, though standardised mortality rates (SMR) (observed mortality divided by expected mortality) are easier to interpret. Mortality in adolescent AN is said to be higher than in any other psychiatric disorder, and is reported to be as high as 15 per cent in some studies. The SMR in an analysis of 10 series was calculated at 3.1 for childhood-onset AN and 3.2 for adolescent-onset AN (Neilsen *et al.*, 1998). The highest mortality was in the first year after presentation in females and in the first 2 years after presentation in males. In females, the risk of death was 2 per cent in the first year, with an annual risk of death of 0.59 per cent thereafter. In males, the risk of death was 5 per cent in the first 2 years and then 0 per cent. More deaths were found to be due to suicide and other/unknown causes and fewer due to the eating disorder than previously reported.

Bulimia nervosa

There are few long-term outcome studies in BN focusing on children and adolescents. Many adults with BN, however, report symptoms starting in adolescence. Outcome studies in the literature are exclusively of females and mainly of adults. A review of 24 studies of BN (*n* = 1383 patients) revealed full recovery in 47.5 per cent, intermediate outcome in 26 per cent and poor outcome in 26 per cent, after a mean follow-up of 2.5 years. A comprehensive literature review found a steady rate of recovery with increasing length of follow-up (Quadflieg and Fichter, 2003). Between two-thirds and three-quarters of women with BN show at least partial recovery after 10-year follow-up. Relapse rates vary considerably between studies. One-quarter of women may still have BN after 10-year follow-up.

There is firm evidence that SMR is raised in BN, but studies have found it difficult to identify a cause of death directly attributable to the specific eating habits of BN.

It is unclear whether age of onset predicts outcome in BN. Vomiting and laxative abuse are reported to predict a poor outcome, and frequency of vomiting seems to be a better predictor than binge frequency. Co-morbid personality disorders (i.e. borderline and Cluster B personality disorders), particularly with alcohol misuse and self-harm, predict an unfavourable outcome. It is unclear whether family features are predictive of outcome in BN, with ambiguous findings reported for those with a family history of depression or alcohol abuse. Unstable family relationships appear to predict a poor outcome.

To conclude, eating disorders in childhood and adolescence are a major cause of morbidity and occasionally mortality. Many cases are 'atypical' and BN is rare before the age of 16. The treatment evidence base is weak, and further good-quality treatment trials, particularly of psychological therapies, will be required to clarify therapeutic components of treatment. Given the role of abnormal cognition in eating disorder syndromes, it seems unlikely that approaches focusing on either family or physical factors alone will adequately address the underlying thoughts and beliefs that maintain these disorders.

2

The role of CBT in the treatment of eating disorders in children and adolescents

Background

'Cognitive behaviour therapy' (CBT) describes a wide range of treatments that emphasise the effects of maladaptive beliefs and attitudes on a child's emotions and behaviour. It assumes that the young person's reactions to events or experiences are influenced by the meanings he or she attaches to them. Cognitive processes are thought to be influenced by underlying beliefs that young people hold about themselves, their future – including their ability to develop into the person they want to be – and others' attitudes. These beliefs or schemata are constructed over the course of development. Mahoney (1991) describes these as lenses which filter perception, cause experience to be processed in a particular way, and affect the way information is interpreted.

How applicable is CBT to adolescent mental health problems?

When young people develop a behavioural or emotional disorder, it is assumed that their cognitive beliefs or problem-solving capacities are impaired, or that they lack the appropriate behavioural repertoires to address their difficulties. Cognitive difficulties may reflect deficiencies or distortions in thought processes. In the field of adolescent mental health, it is often assumed to be cognitive distortions that create problems, reflecting as they do, irrational or flawed attitudes and beliefs. In obsessive compulsive disorder (OCD), for example, these beliefs may focus on the need to engage in rituals because of notions about the consequences of doing or not performing them. Unwelcome cognitive thoughts or images are triggered by negative experience, particularly of a harmful or contaminating nature. Automatic thoughts are generated that enhance feelings of guilt and encourage phobic avoidance of trigger situations. Compulsive thoughts or ritualised behaviours are then utilised to neutralise the automatic thoughts and are reinforced by anxiety reduction.

In anxiety disorders, exaggerated perceptions of danger and fear are coupled with a lack of confidence in the young person's ability to cope with these threats. An anxious child is thought to have developed schemata based around threat – of harm, in generalised anxiety disorder; or loss, in separation anxiety. The subject suffers dysfunctional cognitive distortions and misperceives social and interpersonal relationships, leading to the characteristic avoidance responses of anxiety and phobic conditions. In depressive disorders, the common distortions surround negative beliefs about young people's abilities, their popularity or their appearance.

In general terms, CBT endeavours to assist young people by facilitating the development of new skills (behaviours) and providing them with alternative experiences (gained through behavioural experiments) to bring about cognitive change and challenge established schemata.

> CBT provides a sound theoretical model upon which to base therapy

O'Connor and Creswell (2004) propose a developmental approach to CBT that takes account of a number of considerations, relevant to treating children.

The first concerns the nature of continuities and discontinuities in development. Rather than seeing disorders merely as clusters of symptoms, the developmental approach views difficulties as arising when development has veered off its normal course. The second issue concerns the importance of identifying aspects of children's developmental stage that might influence their response to treatment or determine the way treatment is delivered. Next, the approach takes account of how the child's social context influences his or her affect, cognition and behaviour. In contrast to a more individual approach, it considers such things as peer-group attitudes, including, in our present context, attitudes to weight and shape. A final component of this model emphasises the need to consider continuities between normal and abnormal behaviour, rather than seeing a qualitative difference between the two.

Cognitive restructuring, focusing on the use of Socratic questioning, is used in a range of disorders to modify maladaptive and distorted thought processes. When used in conjunction with social problem solving, relaxation, guided imagery and other interventions, considerable success has been achieved in the management of depressive and anxiety disorders, OCD and behavioural disorders (O'Connor and Cresswell, 2004).

How confident can we be that those as young as 11 have a sufficient level of cognitive development to use the CBT approach?

Paigetian cognitive theory viewed the development of cognition in adolescence as characterised by increased capacity for insight and awareness, described as the stage of 'formal operations'. Gemelli (1996) sees this phase as characterised by the emergence of hypothetical thinking, during which the cognitive capacity for reasoning, processing information and planning the future develops.

It can be argued that a degree of cognitive sophistication is required to develop and maintain an eating disorder. The finding that eating disorders are very rare before pubescence can be seen as indicating that a combination of physical, social and cognitive maturity is required. That is to say, some cognitive awareness of how others see you and how your future might be shaped by life choices is probably necessary to form concerns about shape and how these affect relationships. Furthermore, a belief about how eating behaviour might influence thoughts, feelings and relationships often underlies dieting choices.

One further issue for consideration is whether the behaviour of those with eating disorders is regulated by meta-cognition; that is, the ability to reflect about thoughts and feelings. Whether a young patient is capable of using meta-cognition is theoretically important but may be irrelevant if this is not pertinent to the problem the child is presenting. In this book, we propose that a firm emphasis should be placed on the assessment of each individual child, in order to understand the cognitive processes underlying the child's disorder and the cognitive level at which the intervention needs to be pitched. The problem of what level of cognitive development is required for CBT is not therefore primarily an issue; instead, it is more a question of the kinds and contents of appraisal that are implicated in the generation and maintenance of eating disorders. It is a moot point, then, whether meta-cognitive abilities are required for the form of CBT outlined here, but, in practice, these abilities are generally present in even the youngest patients seen in our services.

> CBT is a suitable treatment for children aged 11 or more with eating disorders

The role of CBT in the treatment of eating disorders

The evidence base for the treatment of adolescent eating disorders is limited. In anorexia nervosa (AN), in particular, little attention has been paid to trials of psychological therapies, including CBT. It can be argued that eating disorders provide a classic example of mental health problems, in which abnormal thoughts and behaviours combine to result in physical and social disability. Cognitive behavioural approaches might therefore in theory be very effective. Although they have not as yet been adequately tested in this age group, results from the treatment of adolescent depression and anxiety disorders suggest that age-appropriate modifications to adult CBT treatment programmes for eating disorders may well yield good results.

Characteristic cognitive distortions

Those with eating disorders suffer a number of abnormal cognitions. Mood disturbance (Herzog *et al.*, 1992), poor self-esteem and feelings of ineffectiveness (Garner *et al.*, 1983) are extremely common. However, the central, specific cognition that is characteristic of AN and bulimia nervosa (BN) is the tendency for subjects to overevaluate themselves in terms of their weight and shape (Fairburn and Harrison, 2003). All other personal qualities and attributes are relegated below the belief that one's self-worth is entirely dependent on either what the weighing scales say or one's ability to restrict food intake in the face of hunger.

The relationship between this central cognition, eating behaviour and physical consequences is at first sight straightforward. The belief in the importance of weight leads to dieting behaviour. Dieting in turn leads to the physical consequences of weight loss. When abstinence cannot be sustained, BN may develop. Binge eating breaks through as a result of hunger and is compensated for by maladaptive behaviour such as exercise, vomiting and purging, which lead to their own physical consequences. Loss of control over eating, with consequent bingeing and purging, tends to reinforce distorted cognitions; that is, the fear of loss of control over eating and weight and also the self-critical cognitions that undermine self-esteem and affect mood.

The physical effects of eating disorders also commonly contribute to the feedback cycle by reinforcing behaviour (starvation increases the likelihood of binge eating, for example), and physical consequences also affect cognition (see Figure 2.1). Weight loss (for those who value it) results in a sense of achievement that is highly reinforcing for those with fragile self-esteem. At

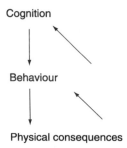

Figure 2.1   The relationship between cognition, behaviour and physical factors in eating disorders

very low weights, starvation affects the ability to think clearly and damages concentration, so this may have an impact on cognition, including the ability to engage in treatment.

> Important cognitions relate to an overevaluation of weight and body shape

The CBT model of eating disorders and their formulation

A number of cognitive behavioural models have been described for the development and maintenance of eating disorders (generally within the adult field); perhaps the most validated one is Fairburn's (1997) model for BN, which has since been adapted to form a 'transdiagnostic' model of eating disorders (Fairburn *et al.*, 2003). This proposes that the restriction of food intake that characterises the onset of eating disorders has two main origins. The first is a need to feel 'in control' of life, which gets displaced onto controlling eating. This need for control may be greatest in those who are constitutionally anxious, perfectionist or lacking in self-esteem. The second is an overevaluation of shape and weight in those who have been sensitised to their appearance, either by prior experiences (e.g. childhood obesity, parental concerns about eating) or by the changes in shape that occur during puberty. In both instances, the resulting dietary restriction and weight loss are highly reinforcing. Subsequently, other processes serve to maintain the eating disorder. In patients who are severely underweight, certain physical symptoms of starvation, particularly the preoccupation with food and eating, heightened fullness due to delayed gastric emptying, and social withdrawal have this effect. In patients with BN, rigid dietary restraint increases the likelihood of binge eating, which in turn encourages further dietary restraint. Self-induced vomiting, while used to compensate for binge eating, results in the binges becoming larger and more frequent. External processes play a part, too. In those who are primarily restricting their eating, interpersonal conflict (e.g. family arguments) and other forms of stress (e.g. school examinations) tend to lead to an intensification of the dietary restriction, thereby bolstering the person's sense of self-control. And in those who are prone to binge eat, adverse events and negative moods may trigger episodes of binge eating, the binges tending to modulate the negative mood and distract the person from the problem at hand.

The cognitive model of emotional disorders developed by Beck (1976), taking into account relevant early experiences, can also be used as a helpful basis for understanding the development of eating disorders in young people. Stewart (2004) has shown how early experience can influence this cognitive model (Figure 2.2).

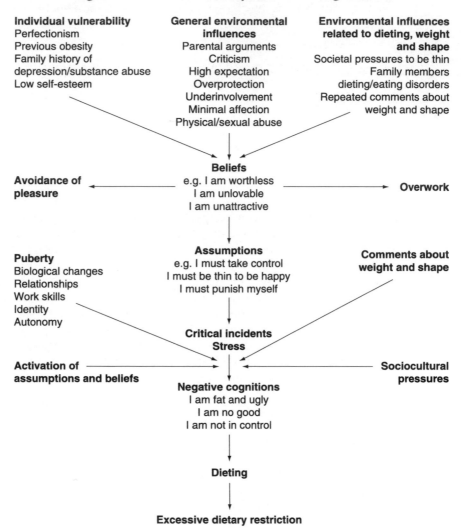

Figure 2.2   Development and maintaining factors in adolescent eating disorders (from Stewart, A., 2004, pp. 363–364). Reproduced with permission of Cambridge University Press

The need to exert self-control is reflected in controlled eating

Diagnosis versus formulation

The current diagnostic systems (e.g. DSM-IV; American Psychiatric Association (APA), 1994) present a multi-axial classification (comprising clinical

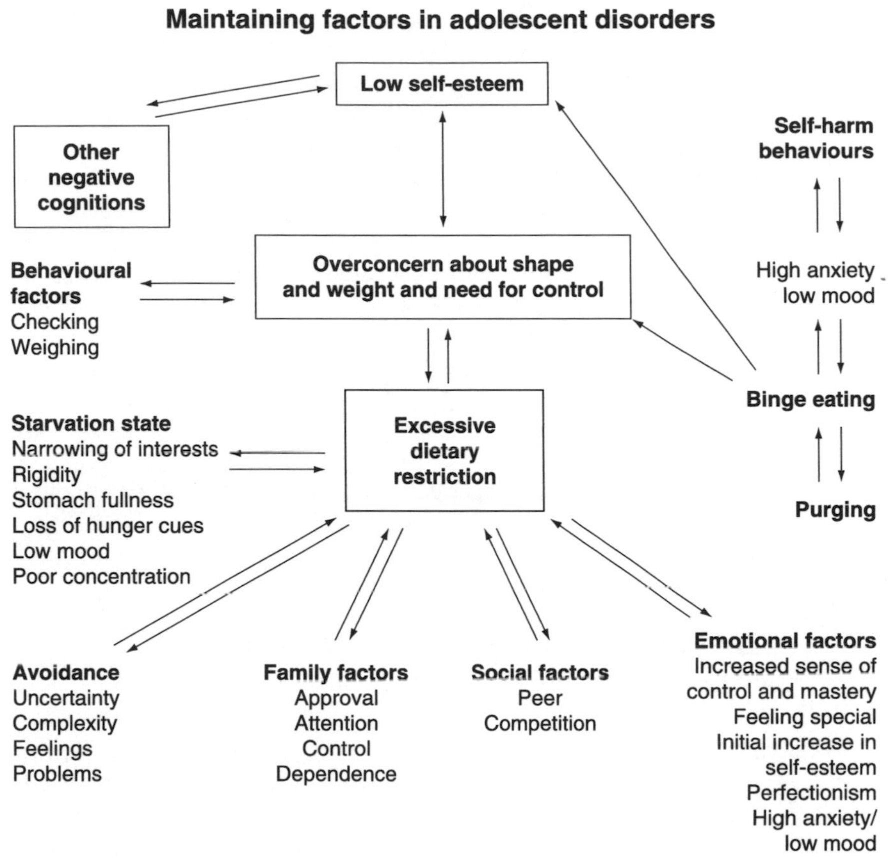

Maintaining factors in adolescent disorders

Figure 2.2   (Continued)

psychiatric syndrome, specific developmental delays, intellectual level, medical conditions and abnormal social situations) and therefore provide for useful communication. They can also be powerful in enabling access to specialist services or additional support. However, they offer a limited understanding of individual complexities, as they tend not to take into account the heterogeneous nature of difficulties. A case formulation model enables moods, cognitions and behaviours that contribute to these types of difficulties to be fully understood. Such an understanding not only enables therapists to treat unusual or atypical problems that may be affecting the eating disorder but also helps them understand and manage more general difficulties that arise in treatment (such as resistance to homework), in the same way that those making up the 'problem' being treated are understood. Because diagnoses are largely defined in terms of symptom clusters rather than underlying mechanisms, they are not helpful in guiding treatment decisions, and therefore we advocate the use of individual case formulation as an essential supplement to diagnosis.

When undertaking a cognitive case formulation with children and ado-lescents, it is important to be aware that cognitions are still in the process of being developed and are influenced by a number of contextual factors, including families, peers and schools (Drinkwater, 2004). Conditional beliefs (e.g. I must be thin to be attractive/loved), arising from core schemata (e.g. I am unlovable) may not become apparent until they have been activated by a critical incident, and for young girls in particular, puberty can be an especially important event. (Indeed early puberty has often been identified as a risk factor for later eating disorders.) If a comprehensive case formulation should take into account both the patient's individual experience and the therapist's knowledge of the evidence, this poses an obvious problem when formulating with a client group with such a limited evidence base. Incorporating developmental models (as opposed to using one single model) is generally necessary with this age group, particularly for those youngsters who hold strong beliefs that predate the eating disorder.

> Case formulations provide a useful way of integrating emotions, cognitions and behaviours

The research evidence base – CBT for child and adolescent eating disorders

The NICE guideline on *The treatment and management of anorexia nervosa, bulimia nervosa and related eating disorders* (NICE, 2004) comprised a review of published treatment trials and systematic reviews with recommendations based on the quality of the evidence elicited. The guideline reviewed all physical treatments, including drugs, service issues such as service settings and psychological therapies.

In AN, although there were a large number of consensus recommendations about assessment and management based on clinical expertise (Category C recommendations), there were no Category A recommendations (across the age range) arising from RCTs. The sole Category B recommendation (based on non-RCT experimental or cohort studies) suggested that family interventions that directly address the eating disorder should be offered to children and adolescents with AN. Although a number of small treatment trials have explored the impact of psychotherapeutic interventions in AN, their small size and other limitations failed to satisfy the NICE systematic reviewers of the robustness of their findings. Most of the research has focused on family interventions. Altogether, quite a compelling case can be made for involving family members in treatment; however, the various studies tend to be small and methodologically different in design, a fact that reduces the possibility of meta-analysis. For example, some studies have an entry point of first presentation at low weight, while others (notably Eisler *et al.*, 1997) entered subjects into the study at the point of discharge from hospital after weight restoration. A number of subjects in some studies have received other concurrent treatments (often inpatient programmes), making it difficult to determine the specific impact of any one component.

A handful of small studies have examined the efficacy of CBT in AN in adults (NICE, 2004). These suggest it may be moderately effective although there is insufficient evidence to date to recommend it over other therapies. Some suggest CBT may be effective at the symptomatic level, as in improving self-esteem, but studies lack power. It is striking therefore that the evidence base for the effectiveness of treatment in AN is based almost entirely on clinical expertise and experience and little on good-quality treatment trials. This led NICE to conclude, 'The treatment plan for a patient with anorexia nervosa needs to consider the appropriate service setting and the psychological and physical management but, unfortunately, the research evidence base to guide decision making is very limited' (NICE, 2004, p. 42).

> **Clinical consensus suggests that family interventions should be offered for anorexia nervosa in adolescents**

In BN, in contrast to AN, there is a much more substantial evidence base and the NICE guideline reaches a number of Category A and B recommendations. Most importantly, CBT for BN is identified as the reference standard treatment (following a number of systematic reviews), and the guideline suggests that this should be offered to adults with BN in a programme comprising 16–20 sessions over 4–5 months. As well as having an effect on BN, CBT also leads to a significant reduction in depressive symptoms. The NICE guideline highlights the fact that there were no randomised trials of this therapeutic approach in adolescents to date, but in view of the apparent applicability of CBT to those in the adolescent age range (with other disorders), it suggests that CBT-BN might be modified for use in young people. These might comprise developmentally appropriate changes to activity planning, including education, and involvement of family members.

> **No randomised, controlled trials of CBT for adolescent bulimia nervosa have been undertaken**

Binge eating disorder is primarily a disorder of overweight, middle-aged people, in which binge eating (not accompanied by purging) is employed to deal with emotional difficulties. It does, however, have quite a high level of treatment evidence, and the NICE guideline makes similar recommendations to those for BN, such as a specially designed form of CBT for binge eating disorder (CBT-BED), self-help approaches, and selective serotonin reuptake inhibitor (SSRI) antidepressants (as an initial first step). It is of note, however, that these therapies exert their effects on binge eating and have a limited effect on body weight. Some overweight and obese adolescents who 'comfort eat' may have this disorder.

Part II

Preparing for therapy

3

Assessment and formulation

Introduction

The assessment of a young person with an eating disorder is a complex exercise which needs to address a number of issues. Firstly, the diagnosis should be made; this should be done by eliciting the characteristic symptoms and behaviours, rather than by exclusion. Investigations should be carried out where required, but the purpose of these in the main is to assess physical complications of the disorder, rather than to make or exclude other diagnoses. For the purposes of this chapter, we will assume that the young person has already received a diagnostic assessment and that the requirement for physical evaluation will have been addressed elsewhere.

At the point of assessment for therapy, however, it is unlikely that all peripheral issues have been addressed and that the way is clear for an unhindered CBT treatment programme to be initiated. There are a number of variables to consider, some of which are general issues familiar to those working with this age group and some are more specific to the eating disorder field.

The first issues relate to the typical adolescents' attitude to attending health services in general. They are very unlikely to have initiated the referral themselves. At the very least, they are likely to be ambivalent about attending and may be completely opposed to it. This opposition has the following components:

- They are likely to be disinclined to attend appointments when they would rather be doing something better.
- Clinics are generally seen as adult/authority settings rather than as something *for* young people, however much effort is put into making them child-friendly. Child and Adolescent Mental Health Services (CAMHS) settings in fact often style themselves with some care to enable them to engage children, but by doing so they may put off adolescents with their toys, pictures and small chairs.

- Mental health services may be seen as stigmatising.
- Teenagers often find talking to adults difficult, and they may have been in conflict with other adults, including parents and teachers, and may expect a negative or critical attitude.
- Young people are at a stage of development at which they often lack confidence in talking to adults or expressing their ideas confidently. Those with low self-esteem will be particularly wary that they will appear foolish, and some may have experienced teasing or bullying resulting from weaknesses in expressing themselves in a school setting. At the very least, they may not expect to be understood.

Then there are issues about the eating problem itself. Certainly, opposition to the idea of referral is common. Although young people with eating disorders are often said to have a better prognosis than adults the latter are more often self-motivated and initial engagement may be easier, at least for those with BN. Very commonly, a parent's concern is expressed in terms that sound like a complaint about the child. The initial part of the assessment can involve the parent listing a series of misdemeanours (dieting, throwing away school lunches, *secretly* vomiting or exercising) in a way which might feel like a particularly bad parents' evening with teachers reporting bad behaviour and performance in school. For the more compliant, perfectionist, young person, this is likely to be something they would actively seek to avoid in a school or other setting.

Young persons' attitude to their eating behaviour is also important. Eating disorders arise through a number of core beliefs that are strongly held; chiefly, the idea that the subject's self-worth (if not others) is rooted in the ability to wield control over weight/shape and eating. Furthermore, if this control is not maintained, compensatory behaviours must be employed either to maintain the desired image or to assuage guilt. Subjects may believe that others (including the interviewer) share their beliefs, in which case they may think the interviewer will be disappointed in them if they reveal their temptation to binge, or alternatively be impressed by their self-control. On the other hand, young people may believe that an interviewer who does not share their beliefs does not understand and therefore does not appreciate the devastating consequences that will ensue if they surrender control over their eating and weight. This is generally expressed as a fear of fatness, but it is frequently a metaphor for other expressions of loss of control. Understanding the young person's attitude and their expectations of the therapist's beliefs is important, as it can determine their attitude to dietary reporting and weighing. Even where there is good engagement, some low-weight patients will want to please the therapist by showing a weight gain, while others will want to impress by weight control or loss. Of the patients who wish to use the lavatory before weighing, the majority are probably water-loading, but a number will be aiming to reduce excess weight to demonstrate their self-discipline and control.

> Ambivalence about seeking help, acknowledging the problem and the need for control needs to be assessed

General principles of assessment

All clinical encounters should ideally take place against a background of the patient's consent. Sometimes this is difficult to elicit at the outset – after all, it is difficult for young persons to provide consent when they are unsure about what they are agreeing to. The young person will often be opposed to the meeting, and, for a younger teenager, the assessment may appropriately commence on the basis of parental consent. Nevertheless, it is desirable to outline the purpose of the interview, clarify the stages and likely timescale, and seek the young person's approval. It often helps to say that the young person's own perspective is especially welcome and that they will have time in the assessment to be seen alone to enable their views to be heard. If, despite these steps, the young person does not agree with the assessment, this lack of consent should be recorded. Addressing ambivalence and limited motivation will be a large part of the initial work before an active intervention can begin.

In a similar vein, all clinical interviews should be conducted against an expectation of confidentiality. This, and the limits of it, should be explained to the young person. The young person should be told that the interview is confidential unless the interviewer makes clear that a safety issue has arisen that needs to be shared with a parent or others. In these circumstances, it is generally preferable for the therapist to talk to the parent in the presence of the young person. Sometimes young people get confused about the rules of confidentiality. The expectation of confidentiality does not mean that they can deny their parents the right to speak to the therapist (and parents can also expect that their private communications are confidential). Similarly, parents can expect advice, which can often be given without disclosing personal matters reported by the patient.

> Obtaining consent and clarifying confidentiality are important issues to address

Multidisciplinary team working

Most CAMHS work as multidisciplinary teams. Moderately severe eating disorders constitute cases of a complexity that would rarely be appropriate to be managed by a solo professional. Some services divide up aspects of the assessment between members of the team – one or more members seeing the parents, for example, while another interviews the young person. We prefer that, as far as possible, all members of the treating team are party to the same information and so tend to work either with a number of team members in the interview room or with some behind a one-way screen.

Conducting the interview

There are arguments for and against different ways of working. The approach is likely to vary a little with the age of the patient, the parents of a 12-year-old possibly being more involved than those of an 18-year-old. The assessment of older adolescents will have much in common with the management of adults, though we still prefer to see older adolescents with their parents, at least initially, even if this is largely to identify the treatment approach and provide support for parents. If we assume for now that the young person attends the assessment with parents, one issue concerns who should be seen in which combination in what order. We prefer to see the young person with their parents first and the young person alone next, followed by joint feedback and treatment planning with everyone at the end. We do not tend to see parents alone, but when we do, this would be before the meeting with the young person.

The joint meeting with the young person and parents

In this part of the interview, it is important to orientate everyone about the purpose of the meeting, who has requested it, the stages, the timescale and the possible outcomes. In particular, the young person should know that they will have the opportunity to be seen on their own and what time the meeting will end. They should know (assuming this is the case) that they will be going home at the end of the meeting. We also find it helpful to separate the issue of psychological therapy from other (physical) aspects of management to some extent. That is, we say that we may or may not make an offer of therapy at the end of the meeting, and that will be something for them to go away and think about – if they want the therapy. This serves the following potential purposes:

- It recognises the young person's views and wishes.
- It enables any therapy to be embarked on without strings attached.
- The young person can take it up as a scientific trial in which they can judge whether it is helpful or not.
- A situation can be avoided in which the therapist's wish for the therapy is much greater than the patient's, and they have an escape if it does not work.

On the whole, paradoxically, young persons are more likely to take up an offer that they feel they have a choice in over one that they are compelled to take up. But separating the psychological therapy from other aspects of management does not mean that the young person can necessarily refuse any aspect of management. Whether or not the patient accepts the psychological therapy, someone may make a decision about the need for hospitalisation on physical health grounds, for example.

> Young persons can choose whether they want to engage in psychological therapy

Seeing the young person initially with their parents achieves the following aims:

- Firstly, it enables the parents to give their version of the history. Generally, we advocate that the parents give the history in the first instance, to avoid putting the young person immediately on the spot and to make a covert statement about power and responsibility. Where the young person has controlled family life to an unhelpful extent, this serves to redress the balance, and asking what parents have *done* to attempt to influence eating behaviour makes a statement about their perceived role.
- Secondly, it enables exploration of the extent to which the child's view of herself and the world have been learnt from significant attachment figures as well as whether there are 'family cognitions' operating.
- Finally, we advocate asking parents about their understanding of the young person's eating behaviour and motives rather than putting the young person on the spot by asking about such things as exercise and vomiting in front of their parents. They may feel compelled to lie if parents are not aware of vomiting, and then it is hard for them to give a different account in the individual interview.

Parents often ask to be seen alone. There are advantages and disadvantages to this. On the one hand, they may wish to impart information that it may not be appropriate to share with the young person. This might include issues in the parental marriage or about a parent's own mental health. On the other hand, it is common for parents to raise things that it would be useful for the young person to hear or which they know about. Furthermore, the young person may be alienated by this part of the interview. They may fear a breach of confidence, and the parents may subsequently believe that they can phone the therapist in confidence during the young person's subsequent treatment. For these reasons, where possible, we tend always to see parents in the company of the young person or see parents for parental counselling (often in a group setting) completely independently of the young person's treatment. This approach is probably most important where there is high parental expressed emotion.

> Where possible, parents and young people should initially be seen together

The interview with the young person

One key aim of this part of the assessment is to gain a full understanding of the nature and extent of the eating disorder. This includes using baseline quantitative measures against which to measure change. These are crucial to the monitoring of progress and evaluation of the treatment, but they also play a part in the therapeutic process. Some of the baseline measures, such as weight and BMI, are relatively objectively verifiable; some might be based on clinician assessment; and others rely on self-report, such as frequency of bingeing and vomiting and completion of self-report questionnaires. Some of the commonly used measures are listed in Table 3.1. When using self-report measures such as the Eating Disorders Inventory-3 or the Eating Disorders Examination Questionnaire (EDE-Q), it is important to feed back scores to the patient. Sometimes assessments leave patients feeling that they are undertaken for the clinician's benefit; it is more important that the young person feels understood, trusted and motivated, and is fully aware of the value of repeated assessments.

An assessment history should cover all of the following areas:

- *physical health*: including weight, height, menstrual history
- *development*: including weight and eating history
- *psychological symptoms and cognitions*: eating-related and other, including mood, obsessive-compulsive, anxiety, etc.
- *eating and related behaviours including compensatory behaviours*: dieting, bingeing, purging, exercise, etc.
- *social functioning*: including peer relationships and psychosexual development
- *family history*: including history of eating disorder
- *educational progress*.

Establishing a baseline and plotting progress over a period of time is important, as those with eating disorders often live 'in the moment'; that is to say, they judge themselves on their *current* weight, or most recent weight change or the current day's rate of bingeing. By taking a longer overview, it is easier to set later change in context and either reassure or identify steady progress.

A further aim of this part of the assessment is to engage and motivate the young person. Where possible, we suggest that the assessment be carried out by the proposed therapist. A non-judgemental approach that accepts the young person's account, rather than a suspicious style, is most helpful. Engagement and motivational approaches are an integral part of the early therapy and will be described further in Chapter 4. However, it is important

Table 3.1 Eating disorder assessment measures

Interviewer-based global measures for assessment and outcome

Eating Disorder Examination (EDE) (Cooper and Fairburn, 1987). A semi-structured interview, yielding subscales of restraint, weight and shape concern, and bulimia

Morgan–Russell Average Outcome Scale (MRAOS) (Morgan and Hayward, 1988). Provides a quantitative score of 0–12 and a categorical outcome measure for anorexia nervosa (good, intermediate and poor)

Self-rating questionnaires

Eating Disorder Inventory-3 (Garner, 2004). A questionnaire covering 12 domains of eating cognitions, behaviours and social functioning. Total and subscale scores can be generated, with satisfactory validity and sensitivity to change

Eating Disorders Examination Questionnaire (EDE-Q) (Fairburn and Beglin, 1994). A self-report questionnaire version of the EDE

Children's Eating Attitudes Test (ChEAT) (Maloney *et al.*, 1988). A variation of the adult version of EAT, assessing attitudes to eating and weight

Other (non-eating disorder specific) measures used in treatment monitoring and review (see Chapter 8)

Interviewer-based global measure of outcome

Health of the Nation Outcome Scales for Children and Adolescents (HoNOSCA) (Gowers *et al.*, 1999). A 13-item, clinician-rated measure yielding a total severity and outcome score and shown to be reliable, valid and sensitive to change

Subject self-ratings

HoNOSCA-SR (Gowers *et al.*, 2002). The adolescent self-rated version of HoNOSCA

Family Assessment Device (FAD) (Epstein *et al.*, 1983). A self report questionnaire designed to evaluate family functioning based on the seven subscales of the McMaster model

Recent Mood and Feelings Questionnaire (MFQ) (Angold *et al.*, 1995). A 42-item questionnaire to rate depression, which has good psychometric properties in clinical adolescent samples

to begin this process by appraising how the young person's life has changed since the development of the eating disorder. Initial exploration of the costs and benefits of such things as self-control, weight loss and perfectionism supports a non-judgemental position in which the interviewer develops a shared understanding of the behavioural choices the young person has made. This challenges the notion that the behaviour is crazy or stupid. Sometimes the patients themselves will suggest that there are no benefits of the eating disorder; in these circumstances, it is sometimes productive to challenge this belief. If the young person is otherwise conscientious and careful, why would they adopt a destructive lifestyle on an impetuous whim? For those who fit the conscientious, perfectionist stereotype, these attributes can be identified as positive values for an approach that involves homework tasks and thoughtfulness. For those who are more chaotic, the discipline inherent to the treatment approach can be offered as a model to bring control back in other areas of life. By the end of this stage of the assessment, the young person should feel understood by someone optimistic of their chances of recovery or at least significant improvement.

> The interview with the young person should be non-judgemental and motivating

Joint feedback session

We propose ending the session with joint feedback to the young person and parents. It is important to allow adequate time to outline an understanding of the disorder and offer a cognitive behavioural formulation without breaching confidential information revealed in the individual interview, unless this is known to the parents.

Case formulation

A case formulation is essentially a hypothesis about the causes, precipitants and maintaining influences on a person's psychological, interpersonal and behavioural problems. A formulation helps organise often complex and contradictory information about a person. It should serve as a blueprint guiding treatment as a marker for change, as a structure enabling the therapist to understand the patient better. A case formulation should also help the therapist anticipate therapy interfering events and experience greater empathy for the patient. (Eells, 1997, p. 4)

Broadly speaking, a comprehensive case formulation has several important functions and these shall be considered briefly:

1   *It should create some understanding of current difficulties and the relationship between them.* A case formulation model conceptualises psychological problems as occurring at two levels: the overt difficulties and the underlying psychological problems (Persons, 1989). The overt difficulties can relate to behaviours, moods and feelings that are interlinked, whereas the underlying psychological problems are usually responsible for the overt problems. For example, problematic eating behaviours and related negative cognitions and feelings about shape and weight may be overt, whereas low esteem or high levels of perfectionism may underlie these difficulties. When creating an initial formulation, it may seem overwhelming for the child if the therapist attempts to incorporate all the available information, and we find that it is helpful to concentrate mainly on the overt difficulties at this early stage. This is generally what

the child herself wants to focus on and is a good starting point. If there are obvious underlying factors, it can be useful to refer briefly to these in the early formulation, not least to let the child know that they will be addressed later on in treatment. However, it is usually sufficient to acknowledge that the formulation is 'work in progress' and will be changed and developed over time.

2   *It should be developed collaboratively with the patient.* Formulations should be developed and shared with the child, to aid the collaborative working relationship central to CBT. This requires attention to therapists' use of language, which should be clear and jargon free. Asking the child what she sees as being the main difficulties and starting with these, as well as using the child's own words as much as possible, can be useful.

3   *It should draw upon psychological theory and the evidence base to guide intervention strategy.* Ideally, a case formulation should be based on a combination of the child's own experiences and the therapist's knowledge of the relevant scientific underpinnings and used to tailor approaches to treatment. Therapists who *do not* draw upon psychological theory and evidence in this way run the risk of becoming distracted from the key issues and are therefore unfocused in treatment.

> The formulation provides an understanding of the child's eating disorder within a CBT framework

The initial formulation

Formulations should be viewed as 'work in progress', presenting 'ideas' rather than 'the absolute truth'; as such, they should be open to modification throughout therapy. Bearing this in mind, it is not necessary, or even particularly helpful, to produce a detailed formulation at the assessment interview itself; indeed, this can be overwhelming for a child who is probably already anxious/ambivalent about starting therapy. However, producing *some* ideas based on what the child has told the therapist is not only a useful starting point for treatment but can serve to increase therapeutic engagement. This is largely due to two important factors:

- It conveys to the child that the therapist has understood something of what she has revealed.
- It creates some hope that change is possible.

For these reasons, we recommend constructing a brief formulation at the first meeting and developing this in the first or second therapy session. We would usually share the initial (assessment) formulation with parents too. When this is subsequently developed, the child is then given the formulation as a diagram to take home and review. At this early stage, we prefer to focus on the overt difficulties; however, acknowledging that there are underlying factors at work, even if this is just a verbal acknowledgement, is important. Ultimately, we adopt the principle of parsimony: the simpler and clearer the formulation, the less likely it is to overwhelm or confuse the child. An over-complicated formulation is likely to hinder any early therapeutic alliance and deter the child from accepting help.

> The formulation is developed over the first three meetings

A bulimia nervosa case example

Therapist: So Fiona, we have talked quite a bit about your eating difficulties and how they affect your life. I would like us to try and make some sense of that by making a few notes based on what you have told me. Firstly, is there anything in particular that you want to change?

Fiona: I really want to stop bingeing and to lose some weight.

Therapist: OK, let's write those two things down: bingeing and weight. Is there anything else that you are unhappy with at the moment?

Fiona: Well, I suppose it would be better if I didn't make myself sick so much.

Therapist: Let's add that. Anything else?

Fiona: I just wish I was happier with the way that I looked – I never seem satisfied.

Therapist: Right. It sounds like, on the one hand, you want to lose weight and look different, but, on the other hand, you are frustrated that this is so important to you – is that a fair assumption?

Fiona: Yes. My friends moan about how they look, but I don't think it affects them in the same way – they seem to be able to eat normally and seem generally happy with themselves.

Therapist: Do you think that you attach too much importance to your weight and looks, compared to your friends, for example?

Fiona: Oh definitely.

Therapist: And how does that affect you?

Fiona: It makes me want to not eat anything, but then I always end up losing willpower and craving food.

Therapist: Let's write that down too. You also talked a lot about how you feel about yourself generally, and it sounded that you feel quite negative about yourself. Would you say that's true?

Fiona: Yes, even though I can be the life and soul when I'm out, it's a bit of a front and deep down, I feel quite down a lot of the time, particularly after bingeing.

Therapist: It sounds like your mood is quite low at the moment and it's hard to know if that has happened as a result of your eating difficulties, particularly your bingeing or if your bingeing has caused your low mood. For now, we'll write that down but remain open-minded as to how it may connect with your eating difficulties.

Once the therapist has made some notes reflecting what Fiona has told her, she continues to increase Fiona's awareness of some of the vicious cycles likely to be operating at the moment. This is an important task, particularly as many patients tend to see bingeing but not dieting as the problem. Fiona is a reasonably insightful 17-year-old. However, younger patients sometimes take more convincing that dieting is central to their difficulties despite this seeming obvious from their description of their eating routine, and it is therefore crucial to encourage them to reflect carefully on their own experience as much as possible. This will become much easier once they are introduced to diary keeping.

Therapist: So far, we have demonstrated that the importance you attach to your looks and weight causes you to restrict your eating. However, sometimes you get food cravings which can lead to bingeing and vomiting. Let's look at this in more detail. What goes through your mind after you have binged and made yourself sick?

Fiona: What a useless person I am and how I'm going to make sure I eat less the next day.

Therapist: Are you ever 'successful' in achieving that?

Fiona: Sometimes, depending on what I am doing or how I am feeling.

Therapist: And when you've managed to 'not eat', how do you feel about your looks/weight – do you go easier on yourself?

Fiona: I suppose I do feel a bit better about myself, but I tend to be grumpy and moody if I'm hungry and usually end up bingeing. I wouldn't say I go easier on myself – if anything, it probably makes me more determined that I can achieve my goal of losing weight if I put my mind to it.

Therapist: So not eating can make you moody, and prone to bingeing but also reinforce your resolve to lose weight? Actually, not eating or dieting seems to be central to your difficulties.

Fiona: Yes, I suppose so.

Therapist: Let's think about your bingeing. Would you ever do this if you couldn't make yourself sick afterwards – for example, if you were in a public place without toilets and it just wasn't possible?

Fiona: Oh no way – that would be way too many calories!

Therapist: So in a funny way, not only is your bingeing causing you to vomit but your vomiting is causing you to binge – because it gives you 'permission' to do so?

Fiona: Yes, I suppose it does.

Therapist: It certainly sounds like your eating is affecting your mood and how you feel about yourself, and I would like us to explore this in the next few weeks. For now, let's draw a diagram to encompass what you have told me so far.

Therapist: *(Showing the formulation)* Does this diagram reflect what we have discussed?

Fiona: That sums up my life at the moment – it feels like one big vicious circle.

Therapist: Well, that seems like a good starting point for us. Shall we try and break some of those cycles?

Fiona: How can I do it?

Based on the above discussion, the initial formulation might look something like Figure 3.1. Note that at this stage, the formulation is deliberately a succinct representation of the main areas of concern for Fiona. The therapist may have some thoughts about additional predisposing and maintaining factors (including family and peer influences), and, indeed, may wish to discuss these in supervision and produce a more detailed formulation, which may be shared with Fiona at a later stage.

As is usually the case, although Fiona felt some frustration at seeing the cycle she had got into with her eating, she felt a sense of relief at seeing this in black and white.

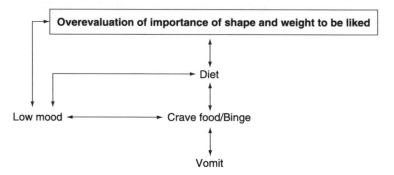

Figure 3.1   Fiona's initial bulimia nervosa formulation

Formulations should be simple and clear and highlight key relationships

Formulating anorexia nervosa cases

The same principles described above apply to case formulation in restricting cases. The main difference tends to be the emphasis on the effects of starvation (emotional, cognitive and behavioural), which the therapist should have elicited during the assessment. Sometimes, children with AN, unlike those with bulimic disorders, are reluctant to reveal any adverse effects of their eating disorder, and in these cases, it is better that the therapist delay the initial formulation rather than 'list' the known side effects herself. This is not conducive to a collaborative understanding and will almost certainly alienate the child. Usually, after application of some of the motivational techniques described in Chapter 4, the child becomes more forthcoming about the nature of her difficulties.

As demonstrated in her formulation (Figure 3.2), a patient, Claire, had a perfectionistic style, and the therapist believed that this was in part due to the high expectations and standards set by her parents. However, at this early stage, the therapist chose not to elaborate on this but rather agreed with Claire that this would be something to focus on later in treatment, at which point, the formulation would be reviewed and expanded accordingly. As is the case generally throughout treatment, case formulations may suggest possible causal factors but should not have a 'blaming' tone. This is a difficult balance to maintain and highlights the importance of emphasising that a formulation represents a collection of ideas to help understand and ultimately resolve the difficulties rather than being the 'absolute truth'.

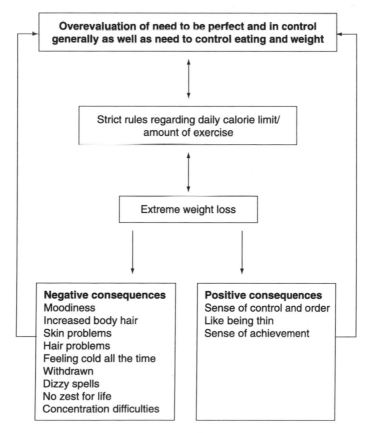

Figure 3.2   Claire's initial anorexia nervosa formulation

> Formulations should include important information in a non-blaming approach

Ending the assessment

After the therapist has presented an initial formulation, it is then the time to outline the treatment programme. This has the following components:

- The first component involves describing the approach and possibly showing the diary and identifying other components such as the place of dietary therapy, parental counselling and progress monitoring.
- The second involves taking a medium to long-term view of the whole programme. The approach is time limited, meaning that we have an expectation of early change rather than inertia or procrastination. On the other hand, the treatment approach is expected to span 4–6 months, so avoiding the unrealistic expectation of immediate recovery. Often by looking ahead 6 months, one can plant an idea, such as 'By your birthday (or by the start of your next school year in September), there is a realistic chance of a big improvement in your quality of life.'
- Finally, there is the 'but'. After we have sold the programme enthusiastically, it is necessary to identify the young person's and the parents' part in the treatment programme. As with so many aspects of the treatment, there are two sides to this message. Unfortunately, eating disorders are not conditions which someone else can cure. On the other hand, this means that patients can retain charge of their progress and pace themselves – as well as taking credit for the outcome at the end!

The parents' and other family members' roles in treatment are described in detail in Chapter 5. The nature of it will vary with the young person's age and the precise nature of the eating disorder as well as its severity. However, the following principles apply across the spectrum:

- The parents should be aware of the young person's treatment, support them in it and prioritise appointments. Some parents will see their daughter's treatment as less important than schoolwork. This idea might need to be challenged appropriately by highlighting the adverse psychosocial outcomes of untreated eating disorders on higher education.
- The parents should be aware of the high expectation of early change, including dietary change.
- They should be aware that their daughter is expected to keep a CBT diary and bring it to appointments, but that this is confidential and should not be shared with family or friends. This is akin to identifying

school coursework expectations. Parents should know of and support the commitment, but not do the coursework themselves!

- Finally, depending on the disorder, but particularly for low-weight AN and where a parent is largely responsible for meal preparation, specific guidance may need to be given about diet. Again, specific detail will be given in the dietetic sessions, but principles such as who takes responsibility for cooking and portion size can be outlined. In short, if a younger adolescent with a severe eating disorder has taken over responsibility for food shopping and cooking for the family, or if she eats only food she has prepared, in isolation from the rest of the family, this would need to be challenged.

At the end of the assessment, we suggest offering treatment and asking the family to go away and think carefully about the offer, rather than suggesting the patient *needs* a further appointment or automatically making one. Although this 'take it or leave it' approach might be seen as engaging only well-motivated patients, our experience is that, paradoxically, the vast majority accept it, as they do not feel trapped or forced against their will. Where the young person is very difficult to engage, we might blur the decision-making responsibility, by suggesting they need to decide together. Again, a positive hopeful, but realistic attitude is often the most productive. It is not helpful to have a lengthy waiting list between assessment and the start of therapy, but an attitude of 'if you don't want the therapy slot, someone else will' is more helpful than a situation in which it appears the therapist wants the therapy more than the family do.

We often suggest a 'try it and see' or 'what have you got to lose' approach with the more difficult to engage. The key, however, is that with an opt-in approach, if the patient chooses to take it up, the therapist has some leverage and can expect change.

After expressing the hope that the young person will return, it just remains for the therapist to await the acceptance phone call and organise the initial treatment, ideally by having the first two or three appointments pencilled in the diary!

4

Engaging and motivating young people

Introduction

Adolescence is characterised by the development of autonomy and personal identity. Ambivalence is common and, not surprisingly, many adolescents are resistant to therapeutic interventions. Indeed, one of the consistent aspects of AN is the denial that there is any problem in the face of an overt signal of disease, such as starvation, and it is this clash of perceptions which frequently leads to confrontation and coercion into treatment.

Why is engagement important?

Coercive treatment (through the use of the Mental Health Act, the Children Act or treatment under parental consent) would be justified if the outcomes merited it. However, while important, short-term physical improvements may be made, there is little evidence to suggest that such approaches result in productive psychological change. It is important to remember that eating disorders, are, after all, psychological disorders, typically characterised by low self-esteem and ineffectiveness, and a coercive approach may serve to exacerbate these cognitions. Clinical experience suggests that in AN, weight gain achieved against the patient's wishes is generally rapidly lost, while in BN, it is not easy to stop someone from bingeing or vomiting against their wishes.

Primary factors affecting patients' willingness to engage with and adhere to a psychologically oriented treatment include doubts about the credibility of the treatment, negative reactions to being referred for treatment, and problems associated with the therapeutic relationship. In the very early stages of treatment (as early as the first session), it is usually helpful to empathise with any feelings of being coerced into treatment and to acknowledge how difficult it must have been to come to the session.

> Coercive treatment seldom results in lasting change

Parental motivation

Often, parental expectations of treatment can be influential in the child's level of motivation. Unrealistically high expectations (e.g. that the young person will quickly be able to give up all eating disordered behaviours and the preoccupation with thinness) can be just as counterproductive as having too low expectations ('nothing will help – I don't know why we are bothering'). The therapist may have the task of working with the parents either to raise or lower their expectations, as both kinds of expectations run the risk of negatively affecting their own motivation to bring their child for treatment.

> *Emma is a 16-year-old girl with binge purging AN. Emma's parents are divorced; while she lives with her mum in the main, she stays with her father every other weekend. She attended her initial assessment with her mother and her mother's new partner, whom she does not see as having an authority role with respect to her. At assessment, her mum was full of hope that Emma would 'finally get herself sorted out' and was relieved that the family would no longer have to cope with her odd eating habits, particularly the bingeing and vomiting, as well as the daily arguments, most of which were instigated by Emma. However, when mum was told that the sessions would initially be weekly at the eating disorder clinic (a 45-minute drive) and that it was recommended that both she and her partner, as well as Emma's father, would need to be involved to some extent (although separate sessions could be arranged for them), she became less positive. Mum felt that the eating disorder was Emma's problem, and so she did not want to 'interfere' with her treatment. In any case, she could not afford the time off work to bring her to sessions. Mum was also disappointed to hear that recovery could take several months to a year at least, and that while it was important to be optimistic and have reasonably high expectations, those expectations also needed to be realistic.*

While the motivation of the patients themselves is of paramount importance, even patients high in motivation may struggle to recover if the parents are not willing to play their part in the recovery process, and this is almost universally true for very young patients. In such cases, working with the parents to change their motivation is strongly indicated.

In other cases, parents may be highly motivated, while their child may not be, but, as suggested above, a coercive approach is likely to be ineffective at best and counterproductive at worst. Assuming the young person's condition is relatively stable and she is not at any immediate risk, the task of the therapist may be to encourage the parents to accept that psychological therapy may not be effective currently, but that CBT will be an option in the future should their child be willing to give it a try. This information can be taken badly by parents, and the therapist may benefit from support from other members of the team when breaking this news.

> Parental expectations about treatment need to be addressed

What is engagement about?

Engagement requires a balance between being an 'expert' while simultaneously being able to learn from the young person. It is important that the therapist demonstrate a willingness to understand the patient's perspective rather than criticise it, and convey a position that is different from that of parents or other authority figures. Conveying the following three messages to the young person is a good starting point in facilitating engagement:

- You are interested.
- You want to understand.
- You want to (and believe you can) help.

The following techniques can be useful in conveying these messages and increasing engagement.

Use written psycho-educational materials

Therapists understandably feel the need to stress the negative impact of the eating disorder, in the hope that this will spur the child into action to reverse their eating disorder. Psycho-education is a central component of CBT and its role in the treatment of eating disorders cannot be overstated. However, launching into a discussion about this at the start of treatment can be counterproductive, and, in the young person's eyes, make the therapist resemble a 'nagging' parent, a situation that is not conducive to a collaborative therapeutic alliance. Instead, it can be useful to acknowledge that the patients may have 'heard it all before' (even though there are likely to be some pieces of information that are new to them) and give them some written handouts to take home. Sometimes, patients appear reluctant to take the information and report no intention of reading it, but, in reality, they are usually intrigued enough to do so. The therapist can revisit this information at a later stage when the patient is more willing to discuss it.

Introduce the concept of a 'higher power'

Often, in addition to being afraid about weight gain and recovery in general, young people have particular anxieties about treatment that make them defensive and guarded and can be problematic for engagement. These might include a reluctance to be weighed or a fear that information may be shared with parents. Typically, when discussing issues of confidentiality (see Chapter 3), therapists will refer to an 'obligation' to report any information about risk to parents and other relevant professionals, thus implying that the decision is out of their hands, a sometimes useful technique in preserving the therapeutic relationship. A similar technique can be used if the patient is reluctant to be weighed: 'In our service, we are required to monitor your weight as part of our role in monitoring your physical health, so let's work out how best to do this.' By referring to a 'higher authority', the therapist manages to avoid confrontation, which can be extremely damaging to the therapeutic relationship.

Learn about the inspirational role models of the patient

Finding out about inspirational figures is not only helpful in terms of providing some insight into what motivates the young person but also shows a great willingness to understand the young person's perspective. Typically, such figures have celebrity status, such as actors or pop stars, and this can lead to interesting discussions about perceptions of 'specialness' – often something valued in eating disorder sufferers. Encouraging patients to think about the pros and cons of being their idol (for example, the specialness of celebrity versus the negative criticism attracted on occasion) as well as identify the specific qualities they admire (e.g. good looks, confidence, power) may not produce much cognitive change at this early stage. However, it should help to engage the patient and provide a basis for some more cognitive work later on in treatment.

> Engagement can be facilitated through the use of psycho-educational materials, clarifying treatment requirements and learning about important role models

Gowers and Smyth (2004) found that positive early motivation predicted early engagement and weight gain in AN, suggesting that this is a key variable in determining outcome. CBT makes no a priori assumption that the patient is committed to change, and therefore treatment protocols are designed to enhance motivation. Accordingly, it is well suited to adolescents who are ambivalent about change or who do not feel they need treatment. The collaborative style of therapy, which explicitly encourages change, respects the adolescent's autonomy while increasing the likelihood that he or she will be an active participant in treatment. CBT shares much in common with the philosophies of motivational interviewing, which evolved from experience in the treatment of substance abuse (Miller, 1983), and it is these overlapping principles that should be used to address motivation in adolescents with eating disorders.

Assessing motivation: stages of change model

The transtheoretical model of change described by Prochaska and DiClemente (1986; 1992) is a theoretical and comprehensive model of change that was initially developed for use in the field of addictions and has been widely used to clarify the therapeutic process and outcome in the treatment of eating disorders (Gowers and Smyth, 2004; Treasure and Ward, 1997). This model suggests that people are considered as being in one of five stages with regard to the prospect of psychological or behavioural change (see Figure 4.1). It provides a useful way of thinking about motivation and can enable the therapist to make appropriate responses tuned to the perceived stage of the patient. For example, discussing the means of change at great length with someone in the pre-contemplation stage may be too overwhelming and encourage disengagement with both the therapy and the therapist, whereas such a discussion may be welcomed from someone in the preparation or action stage. Generally speaking, patients with severe AN (e.g. those referred to a specialist service) are less likely to be in the action phase than patients with BN. However, the situation in BN is more complex and fluid because patients want to stop their binges, but they are much less willing to change their weight-control strategies. Patients move back and forth between stages of change, and thus careful monitoring of the degree of readiness to change is important in ensuring that resistance is not generated by jumping ahead of the child.

Pre-contemplation: The person does not see a problem and is not contemplating any change

Contemplation: The person is able to see that an issue is problematic but also perceives advantages of staying the same. Thus, she may have mixed feelings but is thinking about the possibility of change

Preparation: The person is convinced by the need for change and is planning to do something

Action: The person is actively changing

Maintenance: Change has been accomplished and the person needs to consolidate the change and incorporate it into normal, everyday life

---

Figure 4.1 Motivation and stages of change (adapted from Prochaska and DiClemente, 1986)

Motivational interviewing

Motivational interviewing is a patient-centred, directive method for enhancing intrinsic motivation to change by exploring and resolving ambivalence. It is inappropriate to think of motivational interviewing as a technique or set of techniques that are applied to or (worse) 'used on' people. Rather, it is an interpersonal style. If it becomes a trick or a manipulative technique, its essence has been lost. Essentially, motivation is thought of as a characteristic of the interaction between clinician and patient rather than as something inherent in the patient. The spirit and style are central to the approach and can be characterised in the following key points (Miller, 1994).

1   *Motivation to change is elicited from the patient, rather than imposed.* Other motivational approaches have emphasised coercion, persuasion, constructive confrontation, and the use of external contingencies. Such strategies may have their place in evoking change, but they are quite different in spirit from motivational interviewing, which relies upon identifying and mobilising the client's intrinsic values and goals to stimulate behaviour change.
2   *It is the patient's task, not the therapist's, to articulate and resolve his or her ambivalence.* Ambivalence takes the form of a conflict between two courses of action (e.g. indulgence versus restraint), each of which has perceived benefits and costs associated with it. Many patients have never had the opportunity of expressing the often confusing, contradictory and uniquely personal elements of this conflict; for example, 'If I eat more I may feel physically better, but I will also put on weight, which will make me feel unhappy and unattractive.' The therapist's task is to facilitate expression of both sides of the ambivalence and guide the patient towards an acceptable resolution that triggers change.
3   *Direct persuasion is not an effective method for resolving ambivalence.* It is tempting to try to be 'helpful' by persuading the patient of the urgency of the problem by stressing the benefits of change. These tactics, however, generally increase client resistance and diminish the probability of change.
4   *The therapeutic style is generally a quiet and eliciting one.* Direct persuasion, aggressive confrontation, and argumentation are the conceptual opposite of motivational interviewing and are explicitly proscribed in this approach. To a therapist accustomed to confronting and giving advice, motivational interviewing can appear to be a hopelessly slow and passive process. The proof is in the outcome. More aggressive strategies, sometimes guided by a desire to 'confront patient denial', easily slip into pushing patients to make changes for which they are not ready.
5   *Readiness to change is not a patient trait, but a fluctuating product of interpersonal interaction.* The therapist is therefore highly attentive and responsive to the patient's motivational signs. Resistance and 'denial' are seen not as patient traits, but as feedback regarding therapist behaviour. Patient resistance is often a signal that the therapist is assuming greater

readiness to change than is the case, and it is a cue that the therapist needs to modify her motivational strategies.

6   *The therapeutic relationship is more like a partnership or companionship than about expert/recipient roles.* The therapist respects the patient's autonomy and freedom of choice (and consequences) regarding his or her own behaviour.

Motivational interviewing is designed to increase self-motivation through the expression and resolution of ambivalence

---

Issues to consider with motivational interviewing and adolescent eating disorders

This style of motivational interviewing promotes an equal balance of power between client and therapist; however, children and adolescents sometimes find this assumption somewhat alien and threatening, and adults are generally not seen as peers. Furthermore, young people with eating disorders often have very low self-esteem and dismissive attachment styles, and avoid revealing themselves to others. In this context, the therapist may need to give more structure to the session. Typically, adolescents with AN are wary and suspicious and will form an early judgement as to whether the therapist understands their problems and, crucially, whether she will be able to help. Thus, the therapist may need to reveal some level of expertise in a subtle way.

Secondly, the use of external contingencies can be extremely helpful in enhancing motivation and commitment to behavioural change and will enhance the likelihood of cognitive change and ultimately recovery. It is important, however, that the use of such contingencies is not perceived by the patient as coercive or threatening: Saying, 'If you do not eat your dinner, I will stop you from going swimming' may be counterproductive in increasing motivation. In this example, it would be more helpful to have a discussion with the young person about the physiology of weight gain, in terms of the need for a substantial and sustained energy surplus, and to come to a joint agreement that making exercise contingent on adherence to diet should serve as a useful motivator to eat more and be more conducive to recovery.

Lastly, it should be stressed that this motivational style is likely to be ineffective in patients who are in a severe and life-threatening condition requiring immediate hospitalisation; nevertheless, they can and, indeed, should be employed as soon as the patient is in a more stable position.

Socratic questioning

The Socratic method is used to bring information into the awareness of the patient and promote more rational decision making. This style of questioning does not assume 'correct' answers, but rather should stimulate awareness and orientate patients to a more active thinking mode. Wells (1997) distinguishes between the use of 'general' questions, used to open up a particular area of exploration, and 'probe' questions, directed at clarifying issues, gaining more detail, and eliciting consequences and 'worst scenarios'. Wells identifies five basic requirements for eliciting information:

1   The therapist should ask questions that the patient is able to respond to.
2   The questions should provide a way of approaching a particular goal (such as eliciting consequences).
3   The questions should open areas for discussion rather than close them down.
4   The patient should not feel interrogated by the therapist.
5   The therapist should genuinely seek to understand the patient's experience.

Many young people may respond better to this style than the more traditional didactic teaching perhaps more familiar to them. Therapists should use Socratic questioning right from the start, including at assessment, when motivation to change may be quite low. If the Socratic questioning seems to be overwhelming the patient rather than helping, the therapist may choose to be more direct – for example, pointing out inconsistencies or errors in thinking and asking the patient if she agrees. Ultimately, there should be a balance between Socratic questioning and other, more direct modes of interview, such as reflection, clarification, feedback and education.

> *Claire, a 14-year-old girl with AN, has been brought to an initial assess-*
> *ment by her parents but seems reluctant. The following dialogue illus-*
> *trates the subtle balance described above, with the therapist starting*
> *with a general question about Claire's diet, and then moving into more*
> *probing questions.*
>
> *Therapist:* So Claire, your parents have told me how worried they are
>   because they feel you are eating very little at the moment.
>   How much do you think you are eating?
> *Claire:*   Enough.
> *Therapist:* Do you understand why they are so worried?
> *Claire:*   Not really. Sometimes I think they just want to control my
>   whole life. Anyway, I'm going to get a part-time job when I
>   finish school and go to college, so I'll be able to move out and
>   do what I want then.
> *Therapist:* OK. What do you think will happen if you carry on eating in
>   this way?
> *Claire:*   Nothing.
> *Therapist:* Think about it for a minute; why should we be concerned
>   about your eating?
> *Claire:*   I don't know.
> *Therapist:* Well, I realise you may not know exactly why, but can you try

and guess some possible reasons. I'll be happy to give you my reasons afterwards.

Notice that the therapist is not deterred by Claire's lack of response but instead looks for a tactful and collaborative way of encouraging her to apply some cognitive effort.

Claire: I suppose if I carry on I might lose more weight and my periods might not start.
Therapist: Not 'might' – that *will* happen. What else?
Claire: I don't know. I don't really care about those things anyway.

The therapist realises that pursuing this line is likely to be counterproductive at this stage and may result in a battle, similar to the ones Claire has with her parents. Based on her knowledge that Claire is a high achiever and plans to leave home when she finishes school and starts college, the therapist encourages Claire to think about the impact of her eating disorder on this, starting with a general question, and then more probing questions that encourage Claire to think through some of the consequences of her behaviour.

Therapist: Has your eating affected any other areas of your life – for example, school?
Claire: Not really. Apart from when I'm really tired I have to miss school.
Therapist: And how do you feel when you're in school?
Claire: I used to be fine, but just recently I've been finding it harder to concentrate.
Therapist: OK, well done, you're really starting to think this through. Consider this – what would happen if you continue to struggle with your concentration and you need to miss school over the next few months because of your tiredness?
Claire: I suppose I would get behind and then I would struggle when it comes to my GCSEs.
Therapist: And then what would happen?
Claire: I would have to work really hard to catch up.
Therapist: And what if you couldn't?
Claire: I suppose I would have to stay at school and resit the following year?
Therapist: OK. If that were the case, what impact would it have on you?
Claire: Well, it would probably be even harder for me, as my friends would all have moved on to college.
Therapist: You mentioned earlier that you were hoping to get a part-time job and move out of home – how would that work if you were still at school?
Claire: I wouldn't be able to get a part-time job if I were redoing my GCSEs. I suppose I'd be stuck at home even longer.

> *Therapist:* Now you've done really well in taking the first step and com-
> ing to the assessment today. It would be such a shame to set
> yourself back by not taking this opportunity to recover and
> running the risk of missing out on your exams. Do you think it
> might be worth a go?
>
> *Claire:* I'm not sure . . . maybe . . . but I'm scared . . .
>
> *Therapist:* I understand you're anxious about lots of things but remem-
> ber, you can always go back . . .
>
> *Claire:* I suppose I may as well give it a go, but I'm not promising
> anything.

At this point, the therapist is reasonably satisfied that Claire may have reached her own conclusion that she may have something to gain from treatment and may have started to shift from the pre-contemplation stage to contemplation. Much more motivational work will need to be done in subsequent sessions if she is to move forward.

Typically, patients who are in two minds about recovery from their eating disorder are fearful that recovery somehow means that they will have to 'give up' control, and, to some degree, particularly in the case of restricting eating disorders, this is true. Issues relating to control are discussed in more detail in Chapter 2. While it is crucial that the therapist adopt an optimistic stance regarding the patient's ability to recover, it can be helpful to present treatment as an experiment: '*Try it and see if it helps – you've got nothing to lose but everything to gain. If you don't like the results, you can stop and go back to your old ways.*' In practice, patients usually learn that life without an eating disorder is much better than life with it, but knowing that they can go back to it if they want to increases their sense of control and makes them less fearful about taking the plunge of starting treatment.

> Socratic questioning can be a useful way of helping a young person
> discover the potential benefits of attempting to change

Cost-benefit analysis

Two main goals of treatment are as follows:

- to help patients to stop overevaluating the importance of controlling eating, weight or shape
- to help them learn more adaptive ways of coping with life's problems.

As we know, even when young people with eating disorders have entered treatment, they are often still ambivalent about their desire to give up their eating disorder, and it is therefore imperative to facilitate their understanding of the various costs and benefits of the eating disorder early on.

It is important to give permission to patients to voice the advantages of their eating disorder (despite patients often feeling that the therapist is trying to catch them out in doing so), as denial of this is as problematic as denial of the disadvantages. In encouraging the child to pursue this line of thought, it can be helpful to say something about their positive attributes, perhaps even suggesting that developing an eating disorder tends to arise out of thoughtfulness rather than carelessness. It can be frustrating when patients are able to tell you how awful their eating disorder is and yet, session after session, they do not seem able to do anything different to change things. Dedicating a significant amount of time to discussing the positives associated with the eating disorder may seem counterproductive. However, it can sometimes be an important trigger to a shift in the young person's mindset. Some therapists dedicate almost an entire session to discussing the positives, as, by the end of the session, the young person is often desperate to start telling the therapist about all the bad things associated with the eating disorder!

> *Jake, a 14-year-old boy with AN, had seen a school nurse as well as his GP to discuss ways to overcome his eating disorder but had made little progress. Unlike many young people with eating disorders entering treatment, Jake showed a great willingness to recover from his eating disorder. Figure 4.2 shows his advantages and disadvantages list as discussed with his therapist.*
>
> *As can be seen in Figure 4.2, although Jake had more costs than benefits, the fact that his eating disorder was serving to reduce his stress and helping him to feel more in control was crucial in understanding his lack of progress in recovering. The therapist discussed with Jake the need for them to work together to find out what sorts of situations were making him feel stressed and out of control as well as the need to find alternative ways of dealing with the situations that did not involve controlling his eating or his weight.*

> Identify both the advantages and disadvantages of the eating disorder

Benefits of eating disorder	Costs of eating disorder
• Feel more in control • Stress relief • Better skin • Not called names any more	• No energy • Preoccupation with food • Damage to bones? • Mood swings • Less sociable • More aches and pains than usual • Other football players are getting stronger than he

Figure 4.2   Jake's cost-benefit analysis: here and now

Using different time frames

The example above demonstrated a cost-benefit analysis in the here and now. For patients who seem to be in denial about the potential impact of their eating disorder, using different time frames is helpful, as it not only forces people to think ahead and be realistic about the likelihood of life with an eating disorder but also helps to clarify potential factors maintaining the disorder.

> *Emma is a 16-year-old girl with binge-purging AN. Her mother told the therapist at assessment that she seemed to 'have her head in the clouds' most of the time and would not take advice from anyone when it came to her eating. Emma had aspirations to move to London to work in the modelling industry, hopefully as a model herself. The therapist asked Emma to think about the costs and benefits of her eating disorder not just in the here and now but in 2 years' and 10 years' time. Her responses were recorded in a 3 by 3 matrix (see Figure 4.3).*
>
> *It is evident that the balance of the two columns changes considerably as Emma is encouraged to stop focusing on the here and now and to fast-forward her life to consider the impact of still having her eating disorder in 2 years' and 10 years' time. Crucially, despite reporting several benefits at the moment, Emma reports just three benefits in 2 years' and 10 years' time, yet, in contrast, her costs list gets considerably longer over time.*

This is often a difficult but extremely poignant task, as it can help young persons realise that their goals and aspirations may not be achievable, and that they will be impossible to achieve with the eating disorder still present. It is important to stress that the goal of this exercise is not to encourage a sense of hopelessness in patients but rather to motivate them into making here and now changes in order to avoid the longer-term consequences of their eating disorder. Patients should be encouraged to remind themselves of this exercise between sessions and to add to it as they gain more insight into the effects of their eating disorder during treatment. While just looking at the list can be distressing for patients in the early stages of treatment, often resulting in tears, this is not a good reason to avoid it. Indeed, once at the end of treatment, patients are usually able to look back and smile at their list and use it as a helpful reminder of why *not* to pursue an eating disorder path again.

While this exercise can be extremely powerful in encouraging patients to make immediate changes, sometimes, patients convince themselves that they should put recovery on hold until such a time that the eating disorder is starting to produce more costs than benefits. This is particularly true for younger patients or those with a short eating disorder history. It is the job of the therapist to help the patient see that this is a bad idea and that delaying recovery will only exacerbate the illness and make the inevitable task of reversing the eating disorder even harder. The use of metaphor and analogy

	Benefits	**Costs**
Now (aged 16)	• Stay thin • Feel happier • Look nicer in clothes • Be more attractive to boys • Feel more confident • Hang around with popular crowd at school • Feel in control	• Bingeing/vomiting not nice • Difficult to eat out with friends
In 2 years (aged 18)	• Still slim? • Look good in clothes • Sense of control	• Bingeing/vomiting will be more entrenched and harder to stop • More physical effects of bingeing/vomiting • May struggle to cope with living away from home • May lose friends and not be able to socialise • May put on weight if bingeing gets worse • Confidence will decrease • May affect chance of getting job in modelling industry
In 10 years (aged 26)	• Sense of control • Shows good willpower • Other people may envy slim figure	• Bingeing/vomiting will be even harder to stop • Physical effects of bingeing/vomiting may be irreversible • Probably still living at home – not much independence • Probably have no friends left • Likelihood of weight gain increases • Confidence at rock bottom • Unable to hold down a job • May ruin chances of having children • No partner, as unable to hold down a relationship • Will be desperately unhappy

Figure 4.3   Emma's cost-benefit analysis in three time frames

is helpful here. For example, the therapist might ask patients about an example of something that they were very anxious about and avoided for a long time but eventually managed to achieve, such as learning to swim. The therapist encourages the patient to see that the anticipation is usually worse than the reality and that the positives gained from facing the fear (such as being able to go swimming with friends or swim in the sea while on holiday) outweigh the negatives.

Encouraging patients to think about the pros and cons *prior* to development of the eating disorder can also be helpful in two important ways:

- Firstly, patients will typically refer to having been overweight, yet in the cost-benefit analysis, the costs of being overweight often sound more reasonable.
- Secondly, despite patients claiming that other aspects of life were OK prior to the eating disorder, further exploration usually reveals difficulties. These discoveries are important in enabling a shift from the pre-occupation with weight and shape issues to other issues that may have contributed to the eating disorder.

> Encourage the young person to consider the costs and benefits of their eating disorder over the short, medium and longer term

5

The role of the family

In the history of child and adolescent psychiatry, family factors have often been proposed as having an aetiological role in the development of a range of disorders. Unless we believe that genetic or constitutional factors are responsible for all mental health problems, a role for experiential factors has to be accommodated. In thinking about adolescence, it is hard to deny the role of family variables in influencing development. A multitude of parental factors, such as parental conflict, separation and divorce, or parental illness including mental illness will play a part in how developing young persons view themselves and their role in the world. Parental attitudes (alongside those of other adults, such as schoolteachers and peers) will in addition shape a range of moral, ethical and other values. Issues with particular pertinence to the development of eating disorders might include parental attitudes to weight, shape, eating, exercise and perfectionism as well as any history of eating disorder in parents themselves or their own families. The presence or absence of siblings will also have a significant effect on how young persons view themselves and their future. Elder siblings may act as 'trailblazers' for later siblings to follow. An older sibling may be fat, thin, successful or not, impulsive, out of control, promiscuous, controlled, perfectionist, competitive, bullying or otherwise. She may be the apple of her parents' eye or nearly destroy them with concern. The younger sibling may then aim to live up to the elder's achievements, concede that she never can, or determine never to cause the anguish perpetrated by the older brother or sister. Siblings can also suffer illnesses or disabilities, and this can result in the other children taking mature, responsible roles in their care, or resenting them and inhibiting their desire to bring friends home or their ability to make life choices, such as going to university, in order to support their parents. Many of these factors are non-specific, occur to a greater or lesser extent in all families, and are part of the rich, developmental experience that all children make sense of on the path to adulthood. Those relating to weight and shape or issues of control may hold particular meaning to those who are vulnerable to the development of eating disorders.

The role of family variables is of particular importance because:

- Historically, the notion of the 'psychosomatic family' proposed by Minuchin was thought for a while to identify a particular style of family functioning with a specific aetiological role in the development of AN.
- The idea of a specific style of family functioning has not been confirmed by empirical research – meanwhile other disorders which were thought to have a family aetiology, such as schizophrenia and autism, are now believed to be caused by other factors.
- The idea of a specific family (particularly parental) aetiology is often perceived by families as blaming and destructive, rather than helpful or leading to positive therapeutic engagement and recovery.
- Most specialists believe parental involvement is crucial in the treatment of child and adolescent eating disorders, particularly their taking control of the behavioural management of weight restoration. It is also considered important for parents to gain an understanding of the disorder and how it relates to the young person's difficulties in managing the adolescent stage of development, including achieving independence from the family.
- Although evidence is lacking for an aetiological role for family factors, these have been found to have significant prognostic power; that is, certain family styles, including parents' ability to take control of anorexic behaviour and the expression of emotion, are thought to determine the outcome of the established condition and its response to treatment.

Research evidence for family-based treatment

Family-based treatment is the most tested form of therapy for AN. It is widely thought that there is good evidence to support the use of family therapy to treat adolescents; however, this, to a large extent, reflects the paucity of good-quality research for any therapeutic intervention for AN.

There have been only two comparisons of family therapy with any other forms of treatment. In the first, Russell and colleagues (1987) compared family therapy with supportive psychotherapy in young people at the point of discharge from a specialist inpatient unit *after weight restoration*. The family therapy studied has since come to be known as the 'Maudsley method' (Lock *et al.*, 2001). The number of young people in this trial was very small ($n = 21$), of whom only 10 received the family intervention. The results, however, favoured the family therapy at the end of treatment, and this difference was still there 5 years later (Eisler *et al.*, 1997; Russell *et al.*, 1987). It is of note that the family intervention focused on the need to maintain a healthy weight, whereas the individual therapy did not, and so the difference might not have been due to family variables. The second study involved a comparison of a Maudsley-style family therapy with a psycho-dynamic individual therapy plus a small number of supportive sessions for the parents (Robin *et al.*, 1999). The outcome of both groups was good, both at the end of treatment and 1 year later. Those receiving the family intervention showed a greater increase in BMI than those receiving the individual therapy. However, it is not possible to attribute this finding to the family therapy, as the groups were unequal at baseline, and many of the patients were hospitalised during their treatment. This was especially common among those who received family therapy.

In addition to these two studies, there have been two comparisons of different ways of administering the Maudsley method, either as conjoint family therapy (in which all the family is seen together) or as 'separated family therapy'; that is, parental counselling alongside individual therapy for the young person. The findings of these are also inconclusive, in part because the studies have been small in size and therefore underpowered. Somewhat surprisingly, there does not seem to be evidence that seeing the family together is superior to seeing parents separately from the young person; indeed, families characterised by high expressed emotion seem to do particularly badly with conjoint therapy (Eisler *et al.*, 2000). More recently, a larger-scale comparison of a 6-month, 10-session version of family therapy with a 12-month, 20-session version found no difference in effectiveness (Lock *et al.*, 2005).

A further development in recent times has seen family-based treatment administered to several families simultaneously. This 'multi-family' therapy (Eisler, 2005) focuses on enhancing the families' own adaptive mechanisms and mobilising family strengths. It is generally delivered as a block of several consecutive days' therapy, followed by periodic follow-up days, and a number of different techniques are used in different centres. They tend to all incorporate peer support and a focus on practical issues in meal management, including encouraging the families to eat together. Creative therapies are also widely used, including art and music therapies, the latter involving each family improvising a musical piece, followed by discussion from the other families. This form of therapy is in the early stage of evaluation, but preliminary findings have been promising (Scholz and Asen, 2001).

> The involvement of family members is an essential part of the management of a child with an eating disorder

Difficulties in family functioning and prognosis

A number of studies have suggested that difficulties in family functioning cause a poor outcome in adolescent AN, both in general and as a predictor of response to family-based treatment. North *et al.* (1997) found that difficulties in family functioning (according to the McMaster model), rated either by the young persons themselves or by a clinician based on a family interview, predicted a poor outcome a year later. Eisler *et al.* (2000) meanwhile in their small study comparing the effectiveness of conjoint family therapy with separated family therapy, in which parents were seen apart from the child, found that not one family characterised by high expressed emotion had a good outcome with conjoint family therapy. High expressed emotion in this context refers to negative emotion, chiefly hostility and critical comments that might be seen as demotivating and damaging to self-esteem.

Involvement of family members in support of individual therapy

In this book, we are advocating an essentially individual therapeutic approach, in which the young person is at the centre of the treatment. However, this style of therapy understands and incorporates the essential role of other family members.

The main reasons for including other members are as follows:

- to support the individual CBT programme (akin to establishing parents' support for school coursework)
- to establish communication with parents to enable discussion of progress from all perspectives
- to identify other steps that might need to be taken, such as organising physical investigations
- for meal planning, especially for younger subjects whose meals might be prepared and served almost exclusively by others
- to support siblings, by addressing their questions, and dispel any misconceptions they might have about the origins of the disorder, its likely outcome, and their own susceptibility.

> In addition to family involvement, individual cognitive work with the young person is the core element of treatment

How to involve family members

We have discussed in Chapter 3 the ways family members might be involved in the first assessment interview. In subsequent treatment, family members can be seen with or without the young person. There are pros and cons of each approach. We advocate that, in the main, family members should be seen with the young person, but we have also had the experience of negative parental comments and high expressed emotion appearing to have a negative effect on young persons if voiced in their presence. For this reason, we often recommend seeing parents without the young person in a parent support and counselling group, where they can express their feelings and gain support from others, but in a setting where the potential for breaches of confidentiality (by the therapist) are reduced.

Parents or other carers will generally be actively involved in the young person's treatment. In our approach and particularly for younger patients, we advocate bringing parents in at the end of each individual session for 10 minutes or so, with a more extensive family component every three or four sessions. Each session, it is important for parents to communicate any issues or questions they wish, while the therapist can feed back progress in general terms. Sometimes aims from the individual session can usefully be shared with the parents.

> Family sessions can occur every three or four meetings. For younger children, parents should be briefly involved at the end of each session

Emma was a 16-year-old girl with the purging form of AN. She was moderately underweight, as she tended to vomit after her school lunch and evening meal. She had not eaten breakfast for a year at the time of her assessment, as each morning she woke up with a new resolution to make amends for the previous day's excesses. In her third individual therapy session, she agreed to try adding some breakfast to her routine each morning. She appreciated that, as she had limited time in the morning, eating a bowl of cereal was unlikely to develop into a binge, while reducing her hunger meant she might resist the temptation to overeat at lunchtime. It was relatively easy to make this decision during her afternoon appointment, but she knew her resolve might fade by the morning. She agreed to share the plan with her mother at the end of the session, so that her mother could maintain the expectation without putting too much pressure on Emma. Emma also asked that her mother set out the bowl of cereal and remove other temptations such as toast, so that she wouldn't be tempted to eat more than she felt comfortable with and then make herself sick.

Meal planning is a specific aspect of treatment that parents need to take part in. Their involvement may vary from taking complete responsibility for meal planning and preparation at one end of the spectrum, to just being kept informed of the steps an older adolescent will be trying to take, at the other. It will often be useful for a parent to join a dietetic session and then establish a meal plan which is agreed by all parties and written in the logbook diary.

> Parents need to be involved in meal planning

Encouraging age-appropriate independence

AN often results in withdrawal from social activities and anxiety about a range of normal adolescent experiences. Many young people become over-dependent on parents for emotional and other supports, while parents can become extremely protective, though they often feel burdened by the caring role. On occasion, parents will volunteer that they have not socialised themselves or even taken a holiday for a long time, as they feel they can not leave their son or daughter alone. The individual therapeutic approach is one step to encouraging individuation and individual responsibility. This is then extended by involving the parents in gradually encouraging separation and resumption of social activities. Parental concern usually focuses on the risks inherent in not knowing whether their son or daughter is safe. This can be contrasted with the risks of never encouraging independent development. Sometimes by looking forward, for example, to leaving home to go to university, both young people and parents can see the importance of taking steps over time to ensure that this transition can be managed when the time comes.

> The child's independence needs to be encouraged

Who is in charge of behavioural aspects of the CBT programme?

Behavioural change is at the heart of the treatment approach. The targeted behaviours include social tasks, activity scheduling, and completing homework tasks. Above all, though, eating- and meal-related behaviours are central. This raises the question of who is responsible for the required behavioural change.

> *Claire was a 14-year-old girl with restricting AN. At the assessment interview, her parents were asked about Claire's eating behaviour. They described a typical evening mealtime. Claire would have her evening meal on her own an hour after her parents and younger brother had finished and when she was confident the kitchen and dining room would be clear for her to use. When asked what Claire ate, her parents looked at each other and pieced together what they had each observed. What emerged was an account of what they thought they had seen peering round the door, as if describing the feeding habits of a shy animal they were at pains not to disturb. Claire's mother had seen Claire eating a salad with cottage cheese, while her father had seen her taking a low-fat yogurt for her dessert. It was striking how little the parents were involved in Claire's mealtimes, from the choice of food to its preparation and consumption. Furthermore, though they were concerned and*

supportive, they had not tried to influence Claire's restrictive eating, but merely observed and noted it.

In thinking about the role of parents in bringing about behavioural change, it is necessary to consider the age of the patient, the severity of the condition, and how socially limiting the current behaviour is. In the above example, Claire is severely underestimating her nutritional requirements and losing weight to a dangerous level. In addition, her inability to eat food prepared by anyone else and her need to eat alone are disruptive to the family's relationships and expectations. Her restrictions are also likely to be socially limiting.

In this example, we would advocate that the parents take a significant role in the responsibility for changing Claire's eating behaviour. This involves setting out the expectations and then empowering the parents to achieve them. Setting the objectives includes establishing some principles and then filling in the details. So Claire's parents might be encouraged to decide on changes to her diet, adding carbohydrate and protein, and to prepare one meal for the whole family and help Claire to eat with them. The detail might include specific meal planning with the dietitian. Establishing the objectives requires the agreement of the parents that the aims are desirable and necessary. Where parents have views that conflict with clinicians about healthy foods, activity levels, and social and developmental norms, further work may need to be undertaken with them. Parents will not agree to take on the demands of seizing control from their daughter if they do not agree with the aims.

Commonly, parents will agree with the aims of treatment but will lack confidence in their ability to achieve them. Sometimes pointing out what needs to be done will just add to their feeling of failure. Careful therapeutic skills are required to build their confidence. It is often helpful to talk first about having a high level of positive belief; that is, encouraging parents at least to make clear to the young person what is expected. In referring to 'parents', we are implying that where there are two parental figures, a level of agreement between them is crucial in achieving success. If this is not the case, further clarification of their different expectations will be needed, possibly including exploration of underlying views. Of particular concern is a situation where only one parent attends sessions, while the absent parent (often unconsciously) undermines treatment at home. Often this is because the absent parent feels sorry for the young person; in any case, it is generally worth clarifying whether the absent parent would be in agreement with the approach, and making some attempt to meet them, at least at the start of treatment.

In this situation, parents would be encouraged to set out that they will take responsibility guided by the clinical team for meal planning and that the young person would be expected to eat with her family.

In the initial stages and where the severity of the condition demands it, there might be very little scope for negotiation with the young person. However, in order to engage the young person, it must be clear that, as progress is made, age-appropriate responsibility for food choices will be shared with them, and that in *other respects than eating/weight control*, it is important that they retain (or indeed return to) age-appropriate privacy and independence. There is always some room for negotiation even around food. The most helpful policy is for negotiations to take place in the parental counselling session in the young person's presence, to agree a plan, and to recommend no further negotiation at home.

Other aspects of the behavioural plan, including participation in sports, may also need to include parents. Where it can be achieved, it is good to include as few 'non-negotiables' as possible in the plan. So reasonable participation in games and other social activities can be accommodated *as long as* food intake is adequate as demonstrated by *steady weight gain*.

> Roles and responsibilities of the parents and young
> person need to be clearly defined

Addressing parent's own difficulties or eating/weight-related cognitions

Sometimes parents will have their own mental health problems, such as anxiety or mood disorders, which may be exacerbated or even caused by the stress of their daughter's eating disorder. On the one hand, these may be expected to improve when the young person's eating disorder takes a favourable turn; on the other hand, they may limit the parent's ability to take appropriate charge or set reasonable limits. This may be one situation where the parent may benefit from individual therapeutic help aside from the patient (and probably with a different therapist, but one familiar with the issues involved in addressing a young person's eating difficulties).

Where parents have suffered an eating disorder themselves or have strong views about diets or body shape, specific attention is required. Generally, those who have suffered an eating disorder will be desperate to avoid their children developing a similar problem, but they might realistically feel their experience makes it difficult to set limits and trust their own judgement when it comes to such things as portion sizes and choice of food types. Sometimes a parent has an illness, such as diabetes or hypercholesterolaemia, which requires a special diet and creates an impression within the family that 'dangerous' or 'unhealthy' foods might have a potentially life-threatening effect. Where the parent has had difficulty in sticking to a diet, the notions of guilt and cheating on a diet may also take on a special meaning. In these circumstances, it is often necessary to draw a clear distinction between the dietary needs of a growing teenager and the middle-aged parent.

Jake, a 14-year-old boy with an atypical form of AN, had an obsessional preoccupation with appearance. His father, now 45, had been a very good footballer and squash player, but after a knee injury he had had to limit his competitive sporting activity. Over the past few years, he had gained a considerable amount of weight and was found to be suffering from hypertension at a routine medical at work. Somewhat hypochondriacal and obsessional himself, he worked out in a gym five nights a week and was immensely relieved to find his weight had stabilised with the help of a low-fat diet. Jake had always wished to please his father by following his lead. At the same time, he was concerned about his father's health and didn't want to deflect him from his own diet by eating any biscuits or crisps in his presence.

> Parental mental health problems that might affect
> treatment need to be addressed

Involving siblings

The desirability of involving siblings varies from case to case. There is little evidence that conjoint family therapy with siblings actually improves the outcome for most young people with eating disorders. However, sometimes they will request the support and involvement of an elder sibling, particularly if they find this person easier to confide in than a parent. The chief purpose of involving siblings is to gather information from another informant. Siblings are often able to give a more objective account than either the patient or parents caught up in attempting to cope. The NICE guideline (NCCMH, 2004) suggests that involving siblings benefits them more than the young person with the eating disorder. Brothers and sisters are unlikely to know the likely course and outcome of the disorder unless they are told. They might fear a lethal outcome, for example. They might not know how it is transmitted and fear they will suffer a similar fate. If a young person is admitted to hospital, siblings should have a chance to see the unit and have any stigmatising fears challenged. They may wonder about the cause of the disorder and whether, for example, any conflict or even bullying they had initiated might have played a part in causing it.

> Information about the nature and treatment of eating
> disorders can be helpful for siblings

Part III

A CBT treatment programme

6

Stage 1: planning and establishing principles and embarking on change

Establishing the rules and expectations of treatment is very important to give structure, clarify expectations and 'set the scene'. Although this might sound quite authoritarian, the therapist's confidence in the treatment approach will serve to instil hope, provide reassurance in the face of the patient's fearfulness of change, and ensure that there is a high expectation of change (and that it is ultimately the child herself who is responsible for bringing about change). In general, it is important to start as you mean to go on – clear, confident and optimistic.

A number of the cognitive behavioural approaches described in this book may be unhelpful for patients who are very severely underweight and unable to make simple decisions as a result of starvation and/or severe cognitive deficits. In such cases, short-term medical intervention may be required before effective CBT can commence, but we would nevertheless attempt to embark on attempts at initial engagement and address motivation, as soon as possible.

> The therapist should be clear, confident and optimistic

Timings and structure of treatment and therapist attitude

An individual CBT outpatient programme will usually involve between 12 and 20 sessions, depending on the severity of the eating disorder and associated difficulties. For those with mild difficulties, a briefer intervention involving psycho-education and dietary advice may suffice. For children who are significantly underweight, more sessions may be required, as the process of weight gain and acceptance of a new body shape can be a lengthy one. In the early stages of treatment, motivation is a crucial factor, and it is important not to have too long a gap between sessions to keep up the momentum. Weekly sessions are therefore advised. As the child progresses through treatment, the sessions may be less frequent; however, the pros and cons of reducing the frequency should be carefully examined, and any decisions should be based on the likely impact on the patient's recovery. In particular, the need for frequent sessions should be balanced against the need for the child to develop more age-appropriate autonomy and independence outside the treatment setting.

> Interventions typically involve 12–20 sessions, initially provided weekly

There is a body of evidence suggesting that early response to CBT and other psychotherapies (specifically in the first 4 weeks of treatment) can be superior to pre-treatment measures in predicting outcome in a diverse range of disorders including BN. The role of so-called non-specific treatment factors (factors that are common to most if not all psychotherapeutic approaches) is often reported as being crucial to this early improvement in symptoms, and one of the most frequently cited is the quality of the therapeutic relationship. Some experts argue, however, that while a warm, supportive therapeutic relationship may help the patient to *feel* better, it may prevent the patient from doing the hard work necessary for *getting* better. Essentially, it is the patient's and not the therapist's perception of therapist empathy that is reliably associated with clinical improvement. Qualitative research with adolescent females being treated for AN suggests that an 'expert friend' is perceived as the most helpful characteristic of a therapist. The key challenges for the therapist are:

1   to remain interested but essentially neutral and objective
2   to show empathy without becoming too emotionally involved.

Patients with eating disorders often tell us that they would change their behaviour if only they could think or feel differently. It is important to convey the need for the child to make early behavioural changes *in spite of* their thoughts and feelings, which may take a while longer to change. Indeed, some leading eating disorder researchers suggest that it is the behavioural homework assignments characteristic of CBT and introduced early in treatment, rather than non-specific factors such as the therapeutic alliance, that are responsible for the early treatment gains.

Most of the techniques described in this book can be used for all eating disorders; however, the emphasis placed on particular techniques may vary depending on the individual patient needs. Generally speaking, behavioural interventions aimed at changing eating patterns need to be implemented early in treatment.

> Achieving some degree of behaviour change is an important early goal of treatment

Session structure

Most young people respond better to therapy if they know what to expect in terms of both the treatment programme in general and any individual session. The therapist can facilitate this by explaining the session structure from the outset and then sticking to it throughout therapy. In general, the session should be structured as follows:

1 Introduce the session and give a brief recap of the previous session.
2 Weigh the patient and record weight.
3 Review the diary.
4 Agree on the agenda (include review of any homework tasks).
5 Work through the agenda (prioritising if necessary).
6 Agree new homework tasks.
7 Summarise the session and set the next appointment.

If parents are to be included in the session, a decision needs to be made as to whether this would be more helpful at the start of the session (e.g. to give an additional view on how things have been) or at the end of the session (for example, to discuss plans around diet which may need to involve them), or both.

> Clarify the structure of treatment sessions

Addressing priorities in relation to school and other factors

A common and understandable concern for both children and their parents is the potential impact of the treatment on education. Typically, such concerns voiced by patients can be understood in the context of their difficulties, such as ambivalence about committing themselves to treatment and/or high levels of perfectionism. In addition, parents may raise their own anxieties about their children falling behind in school. The therapist may need to disentangle such issues from other practical concerns, such as having to travel a long distance to the clinic, parents having to take time off work, financial pressures, other family commitments, and so on. Any concerns should be acknowledged and discussed. However, while the therapist may be able to be flexible in terms of appointment times, it is important to convey the need to put the child's recovery first. Having a discussion about the impact of *not* recovering in the longer term (for example, on university plans) is a particularly useful motivator.

Diary keeping

As with all cognitive behavioural approaches, diary keeping is a crucial component in the treatment of eating disorders and therefore should be given careful consideration when planning treatment. The diary can take different formats, depending on the preference of the therapist; however, the main assumptions are as follows:

- It should be kept daily.
- It should be completed in 'real time' and not retrospectively.
- It requires information about *behaviour* (specifically but not solely relating to the eating disorder); *thoughts* (particularly immediately before and after eating) and *emotions*.

There are several issues to consider when deciding on the diary format, such as its size and whether the pages are fixed or loose, and there are pros and cons associated with the various options. An A5-size diary is compact and less conspicuous, whereas an A4 size gives more space to write and seems more compatible to including handouts where appropriate. Having loose pages means that young persons do not need to carry the entire diary around with them all day, but it does increase the likelihood of important information being misplaced. However, having fixed pages in a pre-prepared format may be less flexible and assumes that the treatment will not exceed the planned number of sessions. Lastly, it is important to decide who should keep the diary between appointments – the therapist or the patient? If individual sheets are being used, it is possible for the child to bring these in each session for the therapist to review and keep. This enables the therapist to look through the sheets between the sessions and keep a valuable record of the patient's progress. However, this approach can reinforce an unhelpful belief that the diary is primarily for the therapist's benefit.

Unlike personal diaries, someone else will be reading this one, suggesting that the information recorded is likely to be a combination of the truth and what the patient wants the therapist to know – ultimately, it is a communication to the therapist. However, the job of the therapist is to ensure that the patient feels able to record information as accurately as possible, and to this end, encouraging a sense of ownership of the diary seems important.

In summary, an A4 diary with loose-leaf pages that the patient brings to each session but keeps herself seems preferable. Having diary pages for a time-limited number of sessions (20 is recommended) encourages both the patient and the therapist to focus on the task in hand and reduces the likelihood of the patient 'drifting' in treatment. We use the same 'fixed' column headings for each diary page, which, although seeming a little inflexible, is useful both in terms of keeping recording uncomplicated for the child and for monitoring change. In addition to having a space to record information relating to the actual eating experience (e.g. content, time, place), we include a column called 'thoughts, feelings and behaviour', and use this flexibly during treatment depending on what we want the child to focus on at a particular time. If patients require a lengthier treatment than 20 sessions, this is usually because either they are very underweight and need longer to reverse weight loss or they are doing well but are not quite ready for discharge and would benefit from further input. In both cases, weekly sessions are probably not indicated beyond this point, and whereas a decision *may* be made to continue with the daily diary (either by using additional loose sheets or by starting another diary), it may be that the main focus of the work shifts from daily recording to relapse-prevention work. It should be stressed that *not* doing well in treatment after 20 sessions is not a reason for carrying on with more of the same!

> A diary is an important element of the intervention

We recommend keeping a set of sample diary pages to give to patients to help explain a particular task. For example, we may show a child with BN in the diary page in Figure 6.1, as a way of encouraging her to record as much information about her eating and associated thoughts/feelings as possible.

It is imperative that sufficient time be given to explaining the purpose of diary keeping, preferably after the initial assessment or at the first treatment session. In addition to describing the purpose and procedure, it is useful to give patients a handout containing this information (see Handout 3). In essence, the following points should be conveyed:

1   Diary keeping will help the child to understand patterns in her behaviour and how that behaviour is influenced by her thoughts and mood, and vice versa.
2   Through diary keeping, she will learn that it is possible to have control over her eating behaviour and that episodes of abstinence, bingeing or vomiting generally do not just 'happen' without any warning or for no reason.
3   Seeing thoughts, feelings and behaviours in black and white can help her to be more objective about them and will help her to find alternative strategies.
4   While it is ultimately the child's diary and not the therapist's, it is important to bring it to each session, so that the therapist has as much information as possible to use to help the child recover.

The process of recording behaviour is in itself likely to bring about change. Diary keeping is a constant reminder of the task at hand and makes it less easy for patients to turn a blind eye to their behaviour. Finally, there is a deterrent effect in realising that 'if they eat it, they have to write it'.

Tuesday, 5 October					
Time	Place	Food consumed	B for a binge	Compensatory behaviour (V = vomiting, etc.)	Thoughts, feelings and behaviour
Tuesday, 5 October 8.00 am	Home	Cup of black coffee			Feel tired, but determined for this to be a good day.
10.30 am	School	Diet coke			Want a bun, but going to resist.
12.30 pm	In town	Bag of chips			Feeling good; having a laugh with friends.
4.00 pm	Coming home from school	Chocolate bar and bag of crisps	B		Hungry and bored. Have got loads of homework and not confident about doing it.
6.00 pm	In bedroom	6 biscuits	B	V – tried but no success	Trying to do geography. Not too bad but worried I couldn't bring up biscuits.
7.30 pm	At home	Small portion of lasagna, banana, cup of coffee			Anxious, planned to have binge so I could bring it up to compensate for biscuits, but Mum stopped me.
9.00 pm	Watching TV	2 chocolates			Pleased now that I wasn't sick, but a bit worried. Jeans feel tight.
10.30 pm	Bedroom	Nothing			Don't know if this is progress or not. Not sure if I want Mum to help – I need to do this on my own.

Figure 6.1   Example of diary page

> The benefits of the diary in terms of increased understanding
> and the relationship between eating behaviour,
> thoughts and moods are stressed

What diary keeping is *not*:

- *Merely a food diary.* While food and fluid intake will be recorded, it is important to stress that the diary will also help young persons understand more about their thoughts, feelings and behaviour.
- *An exercise that the patient does purely for the benefit of the therapist.* If patients think that they are only doing this for the therapist, they are less

likely to benefit from diary keeping and will be less motivated to do it regularly. The diary is intended to increase the understanding of both the young person and the therapist.

- *A test.* Patients should be clear that the diary is not intended to catch them out and there are no right or wrong responses. The therapist is interested in how patients think, feel and behave, *not* their views on how they *should* be.
- *A retrospective account of the day/week.* One of the most important things to emphasise to patients is that they need to be writing things down at the time they happen, so they will need to have their diary with them at all times. This is partly because people are not very good at remembering things, when under stress or just busy, but also because young persons may be tempted to edit their past experience once their feelings change.

Addressing barriers

The instructions for diary keeping should be given to patients and they should take a copy home to read again. Any foreseen barriers to diary keeping should be elicited and addressed. Generally, people are willing to give it a try, but sometimes there are misgivings and the common ones are listed below:

- *I don't have time/it will be too awkward when I'm at school.* Reassure patients that you are not expecting 'essays' each day and that an account of their eating along with a few words which describe how they are feeling and what is going through their mind will suffice. Discuss ways in which the patient can fill in the diary as close to eating as possible but without friends having to know.
- *I don't want my parents to know just how bad things are.* Reiterate rules about confidentiality and discuss ways in which patients can keep their diary private. Agree that if the patient identifies anything that parents may be able to help with, you will review this in the session and decide together how to discuss this with the parents.
- *Writing down what I have eaten will just make me think about it even more when I am trying to stop thinking about it.* Acknowledge that this may be the case but that the diary will be beneficial in the long run because the patient will be learning more about the eating disorder and thinking about ways to change. It is not possible to recover by putting one's head in the sand and the diary will keep recovery as a high priority.
- *I am too ashamed to write down my eating habits, and having to show them to someone else will be even more embarrassing.* Acknowledge how daunting this must be, but reassure patients that it is unlikely that they will be writing anything down that you have not seen before and that you are not there to judge them. Unless you have a clear picture of what is going on, you will struggle to help them. Showing some sample diary pages can be helpful here. Whether one makes this point overtly to the

patient or not, this is in part how the treatment works, rather than an unfortunate side effect to be overcome. If the patient is engaged in treatment and honest in her recording, she is faced with a choice – persist with her behaviour, own up and be embarrassed, or change the behaviour.

- *I've done it before and it's not helpful.* Many patients may have kept a food diary or some other kind of diary, but it is unlikely they have filled in a CBT diary like this, and so it is important to encourage them to try it and see, emphasising a 'nothing to lose' approach.

> Identify and resolve any barriers to diary keeping

Encouraging young people to identify thoughts and feelings

As with adults, young people differ in their ability to identify correctly and express their emotions and cognitions. Depending on their development stage, some may experience more difficulty than others. Some young people struggle in their awareness of more subtle emotions such as anxiety and have a tendency to polarise their emotional experience as being either 'good' or 'bad'. It is important that such patients do not feel that the diary is 'too hard' or that they are doing it wrongly, as this will discourage them from using it. It is sometimes helpful to encourage younger patients to use visual representations of mood. For example, a young person may choose to draw a flower when feeling happy or a black cloud when feeling down, the aim being to expand the range of things drawn to help express different feelings, which can later be labelled with the help of the therapist. For therapists working with this younger group, *Think Good – Feel Good; A Cognitive Behaviour Therapy Workbook for Children and Young People* (Stallard, 2002), provides useful tips on how to help elicit thoughts and feelings.

Honesty – the wish to please or shock!

As with any self-report, there is the potential problem of patients underplaying or exaggerating their difficulties, and with eating disorders, a desire to please or shock the therapist is common. This minimisation or amplification of symptoms can be difficult to address, as the young person may not admit to it. In these cases, the therapist should pay attention to any discrepancies in aspects of the patient's account and between the diary and objective evidence, such as weight change, and discuss these sensitively with the patient.

To some extent, the therapist can minimise the child's tendency to act in this way by the attitude he or she presents to the patient and her treatment. As described above, a neutral but interested attitude is best. It is hard to get the balance right between 'it's all the same to me what you do' and showing accurate empathy.

Claire, a 14-year-old patient with AN, used to bring a 'perfect' diary to her early sessions: all neatly written in the same pen, no missed meals or snacks, no mention of any discomfort or fears, and so on. This did not fit with her mother's reports that mealtimes at home were tense and that Claire was spending a lot of time in her bedroom crying. Claire was also losing weight. The therapist sensitively asked Claire about her need to please other people and do things 'right', which she was able to acknowledge. The therapist went on to emphasise that although the diary keeping had been described as 'homework', there was no notion of it being right or wrong but rather that it needed to be an accurate account. The therapist expressed that rather than being pleased at the 'perfect' diary, she was actually a little frustrated because it did not give her anything to work on with Claire, and this meant she did not feel as though she was being much help. She made a joke about preferring to see 'messy' diary entries, with food stains and negative comments that indicated that they were being written in real time and with real emotion. Lastly, the therapist emphasised that she would not be judging Claire, that she wanted to work with her rather than against her, and that it was crucial that she had a clear understanding of the situation.

Claire burst into tears and admitted that she had been playing down her difficulties and trying to please the therapist. Although she was eating some of her meals and snacks, she was throwing lunch away at school and often leaving a lot of food on the plate. It was difficult to ascertain exactly what she was eating because she was writing her diary pages retrospectively at the end of the day. Claire felt great relief at discussing this with the therapist, as she had been feeling guilty for being dishonest, and this was making her feel even worse. She admitted that she had also been feeling frustrated that she was not moving forward and agreed that it made much more sense to be honest in her diary from now on.

Working with patients who overplay their difficulties or who try hard to shock their therapist presents similar but also additional challenges for the therapist, particularly given the quest to remain interested and empathic. While it may be tempting to dismiss these patients as 'attention seeking' or 'melodramatic', it is important to try to come to some understanding as to why the patient feels the need to do this, even if this is not addressed until much later in the therapy. In the short term, the therapist should do the best she can to minimise the behaviour, rather than perpetuate it, and to encourage more accurate recording.

Fiona, a 17-year-old girl with BN in week 3 of treatment, would write vague but extreme entries in her diary, which implied that she was having large binges on a daily basis and drinking alcohol to excess. Some days were missing from the diary, but Fiona would retrospectively report in the session that she had binged all day long. While it was clear that she was indeed engaging in bingeing behaviour and possibly drinking alcohol, her account did not fit with her weight pattern, which was decreasing slightly. Fiona would also write long paragraphs about how terrible things were at home and would report, for example, that she had not spoken to anyone all week, yet, when asked in the session, she could recount numerous positive interactions with both family and friends. Fiona had a tendency to overuse words such as 'always' and 'never', giving an exaggerated picture of how things had really been in the week.

The therapist reverted to the initial assessment and formulation, and, together with the information obtained during therapy thus far, used this to formulate why Fiona might be presenting this way. The therapist recalled that Fiona had referred herself for treatment, without her parent's knowledge, and that while they were aware that she had lost some weight, they were not concerned and, if anything, thought that she looked better after losing a small amount of weight. The therapist also recalled Fiona describing her friendships, saying that whereas she tended to be the agony aunt of the group, she rarely shared her problems with others, as she did not want to 'burden' people. The therapist wondered whether Fiona was using her sessions to vent her emotions in the hope that somebody would understand how difficult things really were for her, despite seeming OK on the surface.

While the therapist thought that there may be some benefits to Fiona's parents being aware of her difficulties, it was clear that she did not want this at the moment. However, the therapist made a note to revisit this at a later stage in treatment.

The main task for the therapist at this early stage was to ensure accurate recording, and it was important to convey this without sounding dismissive or critical, particularly given Fiona's fear of burdening others with her problems. The therapist expressed concern that Fiona was having real difficulty with her eating at the moment and that she wanted to do everything she could to be of help. She reminded Fiona of one of her main fears – weight gain – and emphasised that in order to have control over her weight she first had to gain control over eating, and that this required exact, real-time recording, without any omissions. She asked Fiona to be as descriptive as possible when writing down quantities and gave her some sample diary pages to help with this. The therapist also made a note of Fiona's tendency to think in black and white terms, which would be addressed later on in treatment (accurate recording would also be useful in providing evidence to challenge this dichotomous thinking).

Lastly, it was important to acknowledge how distressed Fiona was feeling, without allowing the session to be 'taken over' by this, which would have been easy, given the amount that Fiona was writing in the last column of the diary pages. To this end, the therapist explained that in order to make the most of the session and help Fiona to move forward, she would be looking for the general gist of how things had been over the week rather than a detailed account, and if need be, she would photocopy the relevant diary pages and look over them prior to the next session. She also encouraged Fiona to read over the diary before the session and summarise the main points herself.

Possible issues surrounding the over or underreporting of information in the diary need to be discussed

Setting target weight ranges and planning for growth

The majority of patients who present to a child and adolescent eating disorder service have at least one thing in common – a fear of weight gain. 'What will happen to my weight?' is a common question asked at assessment, and the answer is rarely clear-cut. In the adult field, a healthy BMI is between 20 and 25 regardless of age, and unless the eating disorder has been present from childhood (or before puberty), it is relatively straightforward to calculate a healthy weight for a particular individual based on premorbid weight and eating behaviour (BMI = weight in kg divided by height in metres^2). With children and adolescents, the picture is more complicated and needs to take into account growth and pubertal development.

For those at low weight (usually those with AN), it is helpful at the outset to draw up a graph, with the planned duration of treatment, target weight and expected trajectory of weight gain clarified. This enables the therapist to explain that the aim is a rate of weight gain that is not so fast that they will be at the target before they are ready, but not so slow that they never get there. Often it helps to set a context around the target, such as 'By the summer holidays or by your birthday, you might be much better than last year'; this ensures that the child imagines and plans for change, rather than that it remain an abstract concept.

Patients suffering from BN generally have a weight within the normal range, although those with larger binges and less compensatory behaviour may be more likely to be overweight, while those with smaller binges and lots of compensatory behaviour tend to be lighter. In most cases of normal BN, weight does not change much over treatment, although a small weight gain is common, and patients engaging in high rates of compensatory behaviours (discussed later) can experience significant weight fluctuations.

As described above, height, weight and BMI percentile charts can be useful in identifying where a child falls, and these are typically used when identifying a target weight range for a recovering anorexic patient.

Decisions regarding target weight need to take into account information from the family about the child's premorbid weight/physical development, family weight history, premorbid eating behaviour, and height. It is advisable to identify a target range, rather than a specific weight, for the child to work towards, and it is important that this range is neither too high nor too low.

The minimum weight should not give a BMI below the 25th percentile, and this should be recalculated as the young person gets older and taller. For those who have been overweight in the past, it is important not to set a target weight range that will be difficult to maintain without significant levels of restriction. Generally speaking, a healthy range would be a weight giving a BMI between the 25th and 75th percentiles.

For underweight patients, it is important to be clear about the expectation of weight gain from the outset of treatment. While patients are almost universally anxious about this, very rarely does this come as a shock to them; rather, it is the *amount* of weight gain needed that is the source of contention.

Claire was 14 years old when she began treatment for her AN. She weighed 39 kg, which at 1.58 m in height gave her a BMI of 15.6. This put her at around the 1st BMI percentile for her age. At assessment, Claire's parents told the assessment team that she had always been a fussy eater, even as a toddler, and this had extended into her teen years. She had not started her periods, unlike most of her peers, and had always been petite. Her mother said that while her side of the family were of average build, her father's side were quite small. Given her history, it was unclear whether Claire's small stature was a result of familial factors or her fussy eating, and therefore it seemed appropriate to identify a fairly wide target weight range. Indeed, it seemed quite likely that Claire may have had a feeding disorder in her early years that later developed into a more typical adolescent eating disorder.

Claire's target weight range was calculated in the following steps:

1   *Work out the BMI equivalent to the 25th, 50th and 75th percentiles for a 14-year-old, using the BMI percentile chart (see Handouts 1 and 2). 25th per cent BMI = 17.9 and 50th per cent BMI = 19.4, 75th per cent BMI = 21.2 (not shown in handout).*
2   *Work out the weights equivalent to the target BMI, using the following formula: Height in m^2 × BMI target = 2.49 × 17.9 = **44.7** and 2.49 × 21.2 = **52.8**.*

Claire's target weight range was therefore set at 44.7–52.8 kg, and it was emphasised that 44.7 kg was a minimum target weight. The therapist explained that Claire's height would need to be monitored every 6 weeks, as an increase in her food intake, and thus weight, might promote a growth spurt that would alter the target weight.

> Identify a target weight and a time frame by which this could be achieved

Monitoring of weight

Once a target weight range has been established, preferably at the first or second session, it is crucial that the therapist monitor this with the patient at each session for the duration of the treatment. Sometimes, patients welcome this, as they are keen to keep a close eye on what is happening to their weight during treatment; some are fearful of this and ask not to be told their weight. Others are ambivalent about weighing but may be weighing themselves regularly outside the sessions anyway. Monitoring of weight is crucial in cases of AN because weight gain is an essential part of recovery, whereas, in cases of BN and other eating disorders, weight monitoring may largely serve as reassurance for the patient. However, given the evidence for migration between eating disorders and the potential risk of losing *or* gaining an excessive amount of weight, regular monitoring is advised.

Overcoming challenges to monitoring of weight

- Do not ask patients if it is OK to weigh them, as you invite them to say no. Tell them that this is an important aspect of treatment and that you will be weighing them at the start of each session. Refer to a 'higher power' – e.g. '*I am required to weigh you regularly as part of our treatment policy.*'
- Explain that while weight is not the only measure of eating disorder severity, it is an important one and therefore requires close monitoring.
- Tell patients that by not knowing their weight, they may be more likely to fear the worst and to restrict their eating based on this fear. Knowing their weight is important for them, not just for the therapist! Facing feared issues is an important step in conquering them.
- Explain to patients that, in order to recover from their eating disorder, they need to become less sensitive to their weight, and avoiding this issue will only perpetuate their anxiety.
- Acknowledge the temptation for patients to make changes to their diet based on a single weight, and emphasise the need to look at the trend of weight change – usually 3 or 4 weekly readings will give an accurate picture. (In very underweight patients, any further weight loss between sessions should be treated seriously, and it is important that therapists convey their concern about this straight away.)
- Discourage patients from weighing themselves outside the session. Explain to patients that it is normal for weight to fluctuate and that the number on the scales is likely to change from day to day and even throughout the day, depending on factors such as fluid intake, whether a meal has just been eaten, bowel movements, premenstrual tension and so on. Emphasise that weight gain needs to be assessed objectively and within context, and that this is best done with the help of the therapist.

Claire told her therapist that she was weighing herself at least five times a day and always after eating. Even though she was committed to recovery and gaining weight, she was anxious about her weight going up too quickly now that she was eating more food and so wanted to keep a close eye on it. Claire's therapist asked her to record each time she weighed herself in the diary and describe her thoughts and feelings immediately afterwards over the next week. The diary was examined at the following session.

With the support of her therapist, Claire was able to realise that her repeated weighing was having a negative effect on her eating. If the number on the scales was higher, she panicked and felt the need to cut back for the rest of the day; if it was lower, she could not help but feel a need to capitalise on this by cutting back and losing a little more weight; and if it had stayed the same, she felt a need to 'try harder' by eating less. This frustrated Claire because her weight was dropping, undermining her recovery. The therapist discussed with Claire her main reason for this behaviour, which was to monitor her weight. Claire was educated about normal weight fluctuations, such as those following meals, depending on fluid intake, and so on, and it was emphasised that judging weight on an hourly basis was unhelpful and misleading. It was explained that Claire's weight was being monitored weekly in the clinic, and that to get a true picture of her weight, it was necessary to look at the trend over a few weeks. Claire was reassured that any concerns about her weight would be discussed with her therapist at each session, and any weight gain would be put in the context of her recovery, thus minimising the tendency for her to panic and cut down on her eating. Claire felt anxious at the thought of having to wait a whole week without knowing her weight and thought that she would 'fear the worst' and so reduce her intake to be on the safe side. A gradual reduction programme was agreed, whereby Claire weighed herself once daily, then every other day, and so on. In reality, once she had realised how much her level of preoccupation was reduced through weighing herself less, she was able to stop this behaviour within a couple of weeks.

Weight monitoring is non-negotiable and should
be undertaken at every session

7

Stage 2: tackling problem eating and challenging compensatory behaviours

Structured/flexible eating

Encouraging patients to eat in a structured but flexible way (Figure 7.1) is an essential goal of treatment, and this should be introduced early, ideally in session 1 or 2.

With underweight patients, the initial emphasis is on both structure and content, and there should be a high expectation that children will need to make changes to both from the outset in order to reverse weight loss and start to tackle their fears about eating and weight gain. To some extent, where to start will depend on the individual. For example, a child who has eaten nothing but a small breakfast for a month will find it very difficult to introduce two extra meals and three snacks all at once, regardless of content, whereas a child who has been eating regularly but only very small amounts will need to start increasing the actual food intake.

For normal or overweight bulimic patients, treatment needs to be staged, as it is extremely difficult to tackle eating as well as compensatory behaviours from the outset. The initial emphasis should be on the structure of eating rather than the specific content of food. Aiming at a reduction in bingeing and purging can follow shortly afterwards. To some extent, the patient has to believe that it is possible to maintain a normal weight by eating balanced regular meals, without resorting to compensatory behaviours. In practice, a number of young people will tackle both structured eating and bingeing/vomiting together because they are naturally less inclined to binge if they are eating regularly. However, this should not be automatically expected of children, particularly if their anxiety about eating more frequently is maintaining a desire to vomit, in which case, the message, 'one step at a time', should be emphasised. This will help to minimise any feelings of failure as well as address parents' frustration at apparent lack of progress, which in turn might reduce the child's motivation.

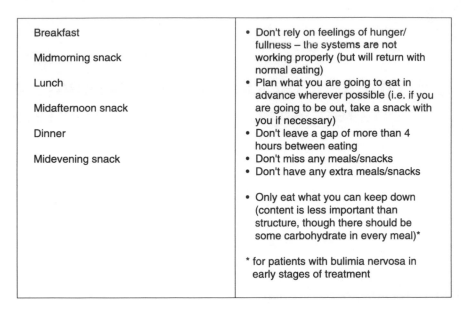

Breakfast	• Don't rely on feelings of hunger/ fullness – the systems are not working properly (but will return with normal eating)
Midmorning snack	
Lunch	• Plan what you are going to eat in advance wherever possible (i.e. if you are going to be out, take a snack with you if necessary)
Midafternoon snack	
Dinner	• Don't leave a gap of more than 4 hours between eating
Midevening snack	• Don't miss any meals/snacks
	• Don't have any extra meals/snacks
	• Only eat what you can keep down (content is less important than structure, though there should be some carbohydrate in every meal)*
	* for patients with bulimia nervosa in early stages of treatment

Figure 7.1   Structured eating

Introduce the idea of structured and flexible eating in session 1 or 2

Compensatory behaviours fuel the bulimic cycle

Vomiting makes people more prone to bingeing and less likely to take control over their diet, so it is important that patients make decisions about what food they can tolerate without vomiting. Secondly, in addition to undereating at meal times, having long gaps between eating is a big risk factor for bingeing, so regulating the eating pattern is an important first step in addressing this. While cravings leading to binges may still occur if the child is continuing to restrict and avoid certain types of food, the act of structuring eating usually helps children feel more in control of their eating, less tempted to binge, and hence less likely to resort to vomiting. Understanding this can increase confidence and is an important motivating factor.

It can be difficult to negotiate a balance between getting things moving quickly and working at a pace that the child is comfortable with. As a general rule, patients recovering from an eating disorder (particularly AN) feel that the pace set by the therapist is too quick and try to bargain with the therapist and parents in order to slow things down. While it is crucial to acknowledge the child's anxiety and to be open to compromise as long as this does not undermine recovery, the therapist needs to maintain a firm stance and encourage the parents to do the same. Motivational techniques discussed in Chapter 4 may need to be revisited regularly during this phase of treatment.

Including dietary advice

People with eating disorders often show an interest in reading about diet and nutrition and are well able to give the calorie content of a variety of foods. Typically, however, the information they receive contains conflicting messages, which can be confusing, and decisions about which diet plan to follow are usually influenced by eating disordered cognitions, such as 'anything with fat in is unhealthy' or 'I must be thin at all costs'. Whereas there is little empirical evidence to suggest a link between media influences and the development of eating disorders, there is much anecdotal evidence that children often read about celebrity diets in magazines and are indeed susceptible to such influences. Sometimes, our patients feel so knowledgeable about diet and nutrition that they are resistant to dietary advice from a therapist or dietitian. At this time, it may be helpful to acknowledge that the patient probably has a lot of knowledge already and that this is a useful starting point.

Discussing media messages about diet and weight can not only be helpful for children in terms of dispelling myths but can also be done in a fun way that can help with engagement. The main aim of this work is to convey that, as a result of the so-called epidemic of obesity, media articles about diet tend to focus on negative messages about high-calorie foods and positive messages about low-calorie/diet foods. These articles fail to address the dietary needs of underweight people, the problem being that these media messages are provided for the many (the overweight) at the expense of the few (the underweight). A healthy diet depends on the dietary needs of the individual. Clearly, the dietary requirements of an active person who is underweight are different from those of a sedentary, overweight person.

Creative exercises can be helpful in encouraging the child to think about these issues in more detail (these are often best carried out as a group exercise – see Chapter 11).

Dietary advice is a crucial component of the treatment, and indeed every session should involve a discussion about dietary intake based on information from the diary. Depending on the severity of the eating disorder and/or the patient's level of resistance to change, an entire session may need to be dedicated to this initially, with frequent revisits to the topic during treatment. Specialist input from a dietitian may be helpful, and this should be utilised if available. To ensure that the dietitian and therapist give the same message and approach treatment in the same way, we recommend that the dietitian be an integral member of the eating disorders therapy team. The dietary sessions should be slotted into the treatment programme as required.

As we have highlighted in Chapter 4, young people with eating disorders are often suspicious that parents and therapists want to 'fatten them up' and encourage them to follow an unhealthy eating plan. This can be a difficult obstacle to overcome, particularly when the young person is surrounded by a peer group who may be dieting themselves. For a successful and collaborative working relationship to develop, it is important that patients feel their therapist is working with them rather than against them, and to this end, the therapist needs to convey a shared concern about wanting the patient to follow a healthy rather than an unhealthy diet. Of course, views on what is healthy may clash; however, the therapist should maintain the stance that a healthy diet should be:

- sufficient to maintain a healthy weight
- binge-proof
- sustainable without the need to follow rigid rules.

In essence, it should be emphasised that any regime that requires followers to go to great lengths to adhere to it and at great cost to themselves is unlikely to be manageable in the long term.

> Dietary advice is a crucial and regular component of the intervention

Planning

In the early stages of treatment, it is likely that the patient's diet will require careful planning, and this will need to be done with the therapist. Depending on the age of the child, parents will often need to be included in this aspect of treatment. For patients with AN, it is usually quite difficult to make decisions about what to eat, and they almost always struggle with any occasion which requires spontaneous decision making or last-minute changes to plans. While a goal of treatment should be to reduce this inflexibility, in the early stages of treatment, this should not be the main focus; indeed, some rigidity is often helpful. Planning the content and timings of meals and snacks can therefore reduce anxiety and encourage a sense of control over eating. For patients with BN, eating is often unstructured and chaotic, and the act of planning in advance can be extremely reassuring for them.

Distraction

Once the plan has been put in place, the challenge becomes sticking to it. In addition to having the list of motivating factors discussed earlier in treatment, having a menu of distraction techniques can also be useful. It is important to devote some time to identifying useful sources of distraction with each individual patient, as further discussion may reveal potential problems. For example, watching television following a meal may be a good distraction for one patient but unhelpful for a patient who associates television with snacking. Similarly, having a relaxing bath to reduce anxiety after eating may be appropriate for some patients but not for those who are prone to rushing to the bathroom to vomit after eating or those who are likely to become preoccupied at seeing their naked body, which may be more bloated after eating.

> Distraction techniques may help young people keep to their structured eating plan

Making eating a discrete experience

A common difficulty experienced by therapists treating this client group is that patients often want to put their head in the sand when it comes to focusing on their eating. Sometimes, young people agree to attend treatment as long as they do not have to discuss their eating. Understandably, patients are concerned about increasing their already high levels of preoccupation with food, and while a goal of therapy is for patients to be able to eat without thinking about it too much, this is an unrealistic aim in the early stages. Eating 'on the move' or while engaging in other activities should therefore be discouraged unless this is unavoidable. This is particularly important for patients with BN, who often lose track of what they have eaten, thereby increasing their sense of loss of control and encouraging bingeing.

> Plan for eating to be a defined event

Introducing 'danger' foods

The notion of good and bad foods varies with the individual and current trends or diet fads, but, usually, foods high in fats are considered the worst, followed by foods high in carbohydrates. The therapist should have a clear picture of foods that their patients struggle with and should ask them to compile a list, dividing the foods into categories of difficulty (see Figure 7.2). It is important that this list be both comprehensive and accurate. It is advisable to be wary when patients say that they do not 'like' certain foods, such as chocolate and chips, particularly when this conflicts with parental and other observations. Ask patients to question whether they would eat the food if it had no calories and no fat in it, and see whether the answer is different. If relevant, drinks should also be included.

Once the 'bad' foods have been identified, patients are encouraged to tackle their fears about them, by introducing them to their diet. Patients may be understandably anxious about admitting to avoiding foods if they fear that the therapist is going to make them eat them, so it is important to explain this aspect of treatment carefully.

Stress that the aim of this exercise is to show patients that:

- They can eat foods that they consider 'bad' in moderation without their

Would NEVER eat	Would eat only if forced followed by compensating	Would try to avoid
Pies	Pastries	Orange juice
Sausage rolls	Takeaway food	Custard
Curry	Croissants	Gravy
Fried eggs	High-fat sauces	Scrambled eggs
Chips	Roast potatoes	Marmalade
Chocolate	Butter	Jam
Ice cream	Lasagne	Full-fat yogurt/milk
Fizzy drinks	Cookies	Rice/couscous
Sausages	Scones	Pancakes
Sugary cereals	Restaurant food	Potatoes
Any sweets	Muffins/cakes	Crisps
Bacon		

Figure 7.2   Danger food list

feared consequences (usually excessive weight gain and/or bingeing/vomiting).
- This will help them to become more flexible in their eating, and that is a major goal of treatment.
- In order to have control over their weight, they need to have control over their eating, and having 'forbidden' foods suggests that the food is controlling them.
- They are much more at risk of having cravings and bingeing (and therefore gaining weight) the longer they deny themselves high-calorie foods.

Some patients may choose to start with the least scary foods and gradually take more risks as they become more confident. Others find that by choosing something which causes them high levels of anxiety they eradicate a whole list of less scary foods in one go. It is important that the patient does not see this exercise as a 'tick list' and think that when they have tried something once they have completed the exercise. Some foods may need to be introduced many times before the patient feels comfortable with them. The therapist should record each time patients introduce something scary to their diet and how much anxiety it caused, until both the therapist and patients feel confident that it can be removed from the list. In doing so, it is crucial to examine the evidence carefully; for example, a patient who would rather not eat chips but feels able to if they are served unexpectedly at a friend's house is less of a concern than patients who will eat chips without protest knowing they are going to vomit afterwards.

> Systematically introduce 'danger' foods into the diet

Addressing compensatory behaviours

The most typical compensatory behaviours seen in this client group are self-induced vomiting and exercising and, to a lesser extent, laxative/diuretic misuse. While the therapist may be aware of these behaviours from the out-set, in some cases, they do not come to light until later in the treatment. This is usually due to shame and guilt, which prevent the child from disclosing them; however, this may also signify a lack of motivation to recover. It is the therapist's job to educate patients about the unhelpful nature of the compensatory behaviours and then advise on a plan to eradicate them. Com-pensatory behaviours promote a vicious eating disorder cycle and greatly interfere with recovery, so they should be addressed early in treatment.

Self-induced vomiting

Educating patients about the ineffectiveness of vomiting on weight, as well as its adverse consequences, can be a useful motivator to stop and should include the following information:

- It increases the likelihood of bingeing because of the assumption that it allows people to eat whatever they want without gaining weight.
- The reality is that less than half of the food consumed in a sitting will be brought up through vomiting, because the majority has already been or will subsequently be digested.
- It can cause significant weight fluctuations.
- It increases swelling of the salivary glands, which can make the face look bloated and round.
- Prolonged vomiting can cause dental enamel erosion.
- It can cause damage to the throat.
- It can cause serious cardiovascular abnormalities through electrolyte imbalance, sometimes being fatal.
- There is the potential for aspiration in young people, resulting in aspiration pneumonia.

> Information about the consequences and ineffectiveness of self-induced vomiting should be provided

Exercise

This may take the form of overt excessive exercising, such as running for long periods at a time but may also be more secretive, such as jumping up and down on the spot in the bedroom or doing sit-ups when no one is around. Sometimes, excessive exercisers feel the need to be constantly on the move, even if this means jiggling their leg while sitting down or clenching their muscles. Whereas some children have never been keen exercisers and start this as a means of weight control, others have always been high achievers in sport, and many are involved in activities such as dance and gymnastics. Whereas a moderate level of exercise is appropriate and healthy, excessive exercise in those with eating disorders (and virtually any exercise in those with AN) is problematic. Warning signs include:

- when exercise interferes with eating
- when exercise becomes compulsive
- when exercise interferes with important aspects of life (e.g. is socially isolating)
- when exercise results in physical health problems (high levels of exercise coupled with low weight can interfere with menstrual functioning and cause musculoskeletal injuries)
- when exercise is driven by unhelpful beliefs about weight (unless I engage in strenuous regular exercise I will get fat) or about self-esteem (I'm not a good person unless I exercise).

Sometimes, education alone can be sufficient to persuade the patient to stop the unhelpful compensatory behaviour immediately, but often a gradual reduction programme may need to be implemented. For patients who struggle to tolerate feelings of fullness, distraction techniques should be employed. Some patients have a set of enduring and unhelpful beliefs that make the behaviour highly resistant to change. These are addressed in Chapter 9.

> Assess whether exercise is being used as a compensatory behaviour

Laxatives and diuretics

Those who misuse laxatives wrongly assume that the lower number on the scale as a result of this behaviour is indicative of true weight loss. In fact, laxatives cause fluid loss, which is temporary and is regained as the body is rehydrated. Similarly, diuretics cause fluid loss through excessive production of urine, which is temporary, and therefore both laxatives and diuretics are ineffective as a means of weight loss. As with vomiting, fluid and electrolyte imbalance is also common with prolonged misuse of diuretics and laxatives.

> *After the first week of therapy, Fiona's diary indicated that she was eating a reasonable breakfast of cereal and two pieces of toast and then would restrict her eating for the rest of the day. Sometimes, she was able to get through the day without eating anything, but on other days she*

was so hungry by the evening that she would lose control and binge, vowing to start afresh the next day. The diary confirmed Fiona's description of her eating at assessment. Although she was having periods of eating very little and she was vomiting a few times a week after bingeing, she had gained 3 kg over the last 2 months. This further fuelled her desire to restrict her eating.

The therapist reviewed the diary with Fiona in detail and discussed the vicious cycle of her restricting-bingeing-vomiting in the context of her initial formulation. This brought the formulation to life for Fiona, and she became upset as she saw in black and white how much she was consuming in a binge and how stuck she had become.

The therapist introduced structured eating to Fiona, who was horrified at the prospect of eating six times a day and was convinced that she would gain even more weight. She agreed that this might make sense for her in the future once she had lost some weight but felt that, for now, she just needed more willpower to diet. The therapist informed Fiona about the likely outcome of continuing to diet, using her past history to illustrate this. She explained that when people vomit they bring up less than half of what they have consumed, and she then used Fiona's diary to show how allowing herself to vomit made her binges more likely. Fiona was shocked to think about how many calories were still in her body following a binge, as she had wrongly assumed that she was getting rid of everything. The therapist used the evidence of Fiona's increasing weight to help her to question this. It was starting to seem obvious to Fiona that vomiting is not a useful method of weight control, and although she was anxious about letting go of this behaviour, she agreed to give it a try. Fiona was still concerned about bingeing, so the therapist agreed to work out an eating plan with her that would reduce the likelihood of this happening. They spent some time identifying distraction techniques to use in the hour after eating and particularly during the evening, when she was most likely to binge.

Dealing with social eating

Eating in public can be a particular challenge for people with eating disorders, especially if the food content is unknown or the expectations of portion sizes are variable and vague, as at a buffet. When helping patients to deal with these situations, it is important to take into account what stage they are at in terms of their recovery, and the particular advice may vary accordingly. Usually, social eating need not prevent the patient from sticking to the agreed plan. If it does, however, as in the case of a patient with AN who is working on introducing three small meals to the diet but is expected to attend a three-course meal, perhaps the patient should be advised to wait until further in recovery before attempting such a challenge. Rather than avoid a special occasion, young persons may need to plan in advance how they will handle it; for example, they might plan in advance to eat a small main course, rather than be faced with a decision on the day.

General advice

- Remember, it is normal to eat a larger than normal meal in many social situations.
- Feelings of fullness after a large meal are natural and will fade.
- The feelings are powerful but they are not evidence that you have gained weight.
- You can eat large amounts from time to time and maintain a stable weight.
- Sensations of fullness are not noticeable to others.
- While you may feel self-conscious about eating in front of others, if you look around, you will probably find that they are too busy enjoying their own meal to be focusing on you.
- You need to eat a surprisingly large amount of extra food to gain weight. Approximately 8000 kcal extra are required to gain 1 kg over and above the normal intake required to maintain a steady weight, or about 500 kcal extra daily, to gain 500 g in a week.
- If you are not sure what or how much to order, use non-dieting friends or parents to help you decide what is a reasonable amount.

Advice for young people at risk of bingeing/vomiting

- See what is on the menu and make a decision about what you feel is OK to eat without vomiting.
- If necessary, see what is on offer and then take some time out (go to the lavatory) to allow yourself time to think about what to eat.
- Leave a gap between courses and avoid eating too quickly. Eating without stopping will prevent you from realising that you are getting full and will encourage overeating.
- You may still feel hungry even after a big meal. Ignore this – your feelings of hunger and fullness are not working properly.
- Distract yourself after eating by chatting with the rest of the group.

Buffets

- Just make one trip to the buffet table (or two if you are having dessert).
- Put what you have decided on your plate and no more.
- Move away from the buffet table while eating – standing next to it will encourage picking.
- When you have finished, get rid of your plate so you are less tempted to go back for more.

> Plan how to cope with eating in social situations

Identifying and addressing 'rules' about eating

Patients with eating disorders usually have a range of beliefs that are so firmly held that they act as 'rules' governing their eating behaviour. Sometimes, these rules are identified in the assessment session, but others may only become apparent as treatment progresses. Sometimes, patients are not even aware that they have the rule. Typical beliefs which are so firmly held include:

- I must stick to X kcals per day.
- I must not eat after 6 pm.
- I must only eat one main meal per day.
- I must not eat between mealtimes.
- I must always eat less than other people.
- I must not eat foods high in fat/carbohydrate.
- If I go over my daily kcal limit, I must compensate (e.g. by exercising or by eating less the next day).

It is a major role of the therapist to help patients not only to increase their awareness of the strength of these unhelpful beliefs but also to see how detrimental these 'rules' are to their recovery. These cognitions can be identified through direct questioning or by picking up on trends seen in the diary sheets. It is useful to begin writing a list of rules in the session, and then ask the patient to complete the task for homework. Once the rules have been identified, they need to be challenged.

Questions to ask

- How true is this rule? (would others share it?).
- How helpful is this rule to me?
- Do I need to hold on to the rule, get rid of it, or modify it into a more flexible guideline?
- How can I modify this rule?

> Identify and challenge strongly held beliefs that act as 'rules' governing eating behaviour

Fourteen-year-old Jake had made a good start in recovering from his AN, in that he was eating regular meals and snacks. However, his weight had not increased and he was still highly preoccupied with food. The therapist noticed that Jake never seemed to be eating anything after 6 pm, and when she questioned him about this, he admitted that this was a conscious decision because he had read somewhere that the body does not burn up food as well in the evening. Together they began to explore other rules that Jake had about his eating. This revealed that although he seemed to be eating more flexibly and had certainly increased the number of meals he was eating, he was making sure that he limited himself to 1200 calories a day. This involved restricting portion sizes as well as food types, rules that had not been obvious from looking at the diary.

The therapist began to explore Jake's rules that he should not eat anything after 6 pm and that he should maintain a daily intake of no more than 1200 calories. Firstly, she gave Jake some information about how being low weight can have an impact on the body's metabolism and discussed how this normalises over time and with regular eating (see above). She then went on to discuss the physiology of weight gain and worked out with Jake how much energy he required just to maintain his weight as well as how much he required to gain weight at a slow, steady pace. This clarified that approximately 8000 kcal were required to gain 1 kg of body weight. If Jake wished to gain 1 kg in a week, this meant he would need to eat more than double his current intake. She also reminded Jake that despite his feeling anxious about it, one of his aims of treatment was to gain weight. Following this discussion, Jake was able to reframe his thoughts and dismiss the rules as being false, realising that they certainly were not helpful to his recovery. Jake decided to replace his calorie rule with: 'I should remember that I need to gain weight and try to eat foods that I do not know the calorie content of.' Jake was still feeling anxious about eating in the evening but could see that he needed to become more flexible with this. He decided to change his rule to a less rigid guideline of 'I shouldn't eat too much food late at night' and agreed to review this with his therapist later in treatment.

8

Stage 3: treatment monitoring and review

Therapists intuitively review progress each time they meet with a patient; however, a comprehensive cognitive behavioural programme for the treatment of eating disorders should involve a more structured review format, with the following three aims:

1   to acknowledge any progress that has been made
2   to understand factors that may be maintaining difficulties
3   to clarify future treatment goals.

It is important that the reviews are not too frequent, to allow enough time for the patient to implement strategies and for meaningful change to occur. However, it is equally important that any difficulties are picked up sooner rather than later, and to this end 6-weekly progress reviews are recommended. They usually combine self-report and clinician-rated questionnaires with a semi-structured interview and review of weight and eating behaviour. Other information – for example, from parents and physical investigations – may also be used. It is important to dedicate enough time to conducting the review as well as to discussing the information obtained from it in order for this to be a meaningful exercise. Generally, an entire session is required for the initial 6-week review, preceded by a homework task of completing any relevant questionnaires; this gives the therapist time to score and analyse the results ready for the review session. Subsequent reviews may be completed in half a session.

> Reviews of progress should be undertaken every 6 weeks

Self-report questionnaires

When using questionnaires, it is preferable to repeat all or some of the questionnaires used prior to commencing treatment to give an indication of change. Recommended measures are described in Chapter 3 (Table 3.1) and are listed in the review checklist (Figure 8.1). It is important to stress the purpose of questionnaires to the young person, and while there are rarely objections to completing them, it is useful to be prepared for the following objections.

1   *I've already filled these in – what's the point of my doing them again?* Many patients will see completing questionnaires as being for the therapist's rather than their own benefit. It is important to clarify that they should be aware of any change, not least so they can appraise the benefits against the costs of any changes they have made. Stress that as a therapist, you are interested in *change*, either positive or negative, and that it would be negligent of you not to monitor this on a regular basis. It is also a useful way of helping patients to focus their thoughts and understand how things are for them at the moment. Many patients will lose sight of how far they have come, or else overevaluate one recent bad day without setting it in the context of several more positive weeks. Explain that you do not want patients to try to remember how they responded last time but rather to describe how they are feeling at the moment or in the last 2 weeks as appropriate.

2   *There's no point in my filling these in because nobody will take any notice of what I say anyway.* Explain that during treatment, there is much information for both the patient and the therapist to assimilate and that sometimes it may feel as though there is not enough time to address everything. Stress that the questionnaires are an important part of information sharing between the therapist and patient, and therefore a whole session will be dedicated to discussing the information obtained from the questionnaires as well as other information obtained during the 6-weekly reviews. This information will enable them both to take stock and guide future treatment.

3   *The questionnaire responses suggest that everything is fine despite the patient's presentation suggesting otherwise.* It is important to be aware that completing a questionnaire is a means of communication and therefore represents what children choose to convey at any time. Depending on whether they want to please therapists or are angry with them, they may want to communicate a particular message. Although an honest, trusting approach should be encouraged, the therapist can use the way the child answers the questions to explore such things as risk taking and challenging adults.

Sometimes, acknowledging any discrepancy can be sufficient to reassure the child that you are being an observant and caring therapist; however, a mismatch between information from self-report measures and behavioural observations of the child may suggest that the child is not well engaged with treatment and/or the therapist, and this may need addressing more directly (see below). The child may also be concerned that the information from the questionnaires may be passed on to her parents; indeed, some parents assume that this will be the case and may even see the questionnaires as a 'joint effort' between themselves and their child. In such cases, it is important to emphasise that the questionnaires are for the child to fill in independently, and, to reiterate confidentiality issues. As suggested above, the questionnaire responses and, to some extent, the diary entries are ultimately a communication to the therapist, and it is therefore crucial for the therapist to try to understand what is being communicated, rather than merely ascertaining whether the information is accurate or not. Guilt may underlie a difficulty in acknowledging certain cognitions or compensatory behaviours. Some patients will score persistently very highly on questionnaires, as if wanting to impress on the therapist the extent of their suffering, or else out of a perfectionist wish to be the most severe case in the clinic. In such cases, change is as important as the absolute score, as different patients will operate different thresholds.

> Self-report questionnaires are a helpful way of assessing change in the young person, over time

Semi-structured interviews

The semi-structured interview involves an informal and brief discussion of what has been achieved in treatment and what still needs addressing. It should be explained to patients that some of the questions will relate to areas that they have been working on directly, whereas others will relate to areas not yet tackled and which may still be quite problematic. The therapist should encourage patients to attribute any positive changes to their own efforts to recover, and should reassure them that as well as continuing work on those areas, you will be addressing additional relevant difficulties in the next phase of treatment.

The content should be broad and based on typical eating disorder symptoms and behaviours occurring in this client group. The interview should be tailor-made to the individual, using relevant prompt questions, which should take into account information received at the assessment and in early diary pages. A rating of 0–5 is helpful in giving an overall picture of the degree to which each item is a problem (5 being most severe). This rating should be made by the patient. However, if the therapist feels that patients are underplaying their difficulties (for example, in the case of somebody with severe restricting behaviour giving an eating behaviour rating of 0), a more realistic rating should be encouraged. Below is a list of sample questions.

Box 8.1 Sample questions

Eating behaviour (score 0–5)
(To include restricting, bingeing, food avoidance, lack of structure)

How has your eating changed over the last 6 weeks?
Prompt examples:

- Looking back at your early diary entries, you had stopped eating breakfast or lunch apart from occasionally at the weekend, whereas your eating seems much more structured now. What have been the main changes for you?

- When you first came for treatment, you told me that you could not eat chocolate, cakes, biscuits or crisps because you feared you would lose control and not be able to stop eating them – do you think that is still the case?

Compensatory behaviours (score 0–5)

Apart from restricting your eating, what sorts of other behaviours are you engaging in to control your weight/eating?
(To include vomiting, laxative misuse, diuretics, water tablets, exercise, and fluid consumption)

Prompt examples:

- You were vomiting up to three times a day when you began treatment. However, your diary suggests that you have been able to reduce this significantly. How much of a problem do you think this is at the moment?

- I know you have always been keen on exercising, but recently you have felt compelled to exercise first thing in the morning and last thing at night, and we have been working on reducing this – how is that going?

Rules for eating (score 0–5)
(To include timings, amounts, places)

Do you have any rules or routines that govern your eating?
Prompt examples:

- I've noticed from your diary that you never seem to eat after 7 pm – is this just a coincidence or is it something that you consciously try to stick to?

- Some people have strict rules regarding their eating that become habits – for example, always needing to leave something on the plate or always eating less than other people – do you think you have any such rules?

Preoccupation (score 0–5)

How much does your eating and/or weight and shape play on your mind?
(Ask about eating, food, weight and shape and assess how much the preoccupation is interfering with everyday functioning)

Prompt examples:

- You told me at assessment that you were 'obsessed' by food to the point of not being able to concentrate on your schoolwork. Is that still the case or has it improved at all?

- Some people find that they are so preoccupied that they cannot even sit through a television programme or have an in-depth conversation without having intrusive thoughts about how they look or what their weight is – does this ever happen to you?

Checking behaviours (score 0–5) How much time do you spend checking your weight against others, or checking the tightness or appearance of clothes? (To include: mirror checking, weighing, camouflaging, comparing, pinching and avoidance)

Do you find yourself going to great lengths in order to reassure yourself about your weight/shape?

Prompt examples:

- Some people are so anxious about gaining weight too quickly and their shape changing that they constantly scrutinise themselves in the mirror to make sure that they haven't changed too much – do you do anything like this?

- Some people are so self-conscious about their appearance that they wear lots of baggy layers, even in hot weather, so that other people can't see their body. Is this something that you do?

Physical health (score 0–5)

How would you describe your physical health at the moment? (Ask about any physical complaints identified at assessment or earlier in treatment (including starvation symptoms) and give feedback regarding any physical investigations, such as blood results.) The weight chart should also be reviewed as an indication of physical progress.

Prompt examples:

- At the start of treatment, you described feeling cold a lot of the time, and you were having lots of dizzy spells – has this changed at all?

- You have made great progress in increasing your eating and reducing your fluid intake, and your recent blood tests indicate that your sodium level is back to normal. However, you had been feeling constipated and getting stomach cramps – how are you feeling at the moment?

General functioning (score 0–5) (To include mood, school, home life, social life, relationships)

Prompt examples:

- You seemed quite down and withdrawn when you began treatment and were spending a lot of time in your room alone. Has this changed over the last few weeks?

> - You had stopped attending school completely when you came for your initial assessment but have recently gone back, which was a difficult step for you. How is this going?

Obstacles to progress

The reasons for lack of progress are often multi-faceted and overlapping. The seven points below summarise the typical barriers to progress for this client group, and these can be used as a checklist to guide assessment and move treatment forward.

Environmental/external factors

These can relate to the practical situation of the patient as well as inter-personal difficulties. School- and family-related problems as well as competitive peer relationships (common in this age group) are typical factors which impede recovery. Peer relationship issues include dieting within the peer group and competitive exam situations, which may exacerbate any perfectionist or control-seeking tendency.

Eating disorder symptoms/behaviours

While some of these will hopefully have been addressed already in treatment, some may remain, either because they have not yet been tackled much in treatment (e.g. overevaluation of the importance of controlling eating) or because the patient is struggling to address them (e.g. dieting).

Mood

Patients who present with eating disorders, particularly AN, often describe symptoms of low mood, and this is usually reversed with more flexible eating and an increase in weight. However, for some, low mood continues after weight gain and interferes with functioning to the point where progress seems unlikely unless there is a significant improvement in mood first. This may need addressing through a shift in CBT focus.

Motivation

For a CBT approach to stand a chance of being effective, some degree of motivation is essential, and yet, as described elsewhere in this book, many of our patients begin treatment with limited, if any, motivation to change; hence, the emphasis on addressing this from the outset. If motivation remains poor after 6 weeks of treatment and onwards, it signifies a major problem in terms of the patient's recovery, and a clear understanding of why the child feels unmotivated is crucial. Factors affecting motivation have been described in Chapter 4. Generally speaking, lack of motivation falls into two main categories:

1 not wanting to change
2 wanting to change but not feeling able to do so.

Usually, lack of motivation involves a combination of the two, resulting in ambivalence.

Cognitive style

Most people with eating disorders show unhelpful biases in their thinking or have specific thoughts which serve to maintain their disorder. For some, this is exacerbated by a more general unhelpful style of thinking, such as a tendency to evaluate situations in an all or nothing way. These styles are discussed in more detail in Chapter 9. The therapist should begin to gather information about the child's thinking style from the outset of the treatment.

Unrealistic/perfectionist standards

Having unrealistic expectations about change will interfere with recovery, and these are common in patients who are high achievers and have perfectionist standards. They are more commonly seen in patients with AN, as discussed in Chapter 9.

Treatment/therapist

Generally speaking, problems in implementing the treatment are the result of a combination of factors, but sometimes, the difficulties are inherent within the therapy or the therapist. For example, it may be that the child does not agree with the cognitive behavioural model, or that the treatment is not being carried out competently. There may also be difficulties in the therapist–patient relationship that need to be addressed if treatment is to stand a chance of being effective.

> Claire, a 14-year-old girl suffering from AN, had completed six weekly sessions of the treatment programme and had managed to make some positive changes to her eating, in that she was able to eat three meals and a couple of snacks daily and was gradually introducing foods she classed as 'scary', such as non-sugary cereals and the occasional chocolate biscuit. She continued to express concerns about her weight and shape in her diary pages and often wrote about arguments at home. Physically, she remained underweight, having gained just 2 kg, and she was still not menstruating.

Information source	Obstacles to progress					
	Eating disorder symptoms	Motivation	Mood	Family/social difficulties	Treatment/ therapist	Cognitive style
Diary	*	*	*	*	*	*
Therapist	*	*	*	*	*	*
Interview	*	*	*	*	*	*
Parents	*		*	*	*	*
Eating Disorders Inventory-3	*					
Family Assessment Device				*		
HoNOSCA and HoNOSCA-SR	*		*	*		
Recent Mood and Feeling Questionnaire			*			
Motivation Q		*			*	
Physical assessment	*					

Figure 8.1   Review checklist (see Chapter 3 for details)

At session 6, Claire's therapist explained that they would be spending most of the session discussing what had been achieved so far in treatment and what still needed addressing. Using the prompt questions from the semi-structured interview, the therapist was able to encourage Claire to talk about the positive changes she had made with her eating. This was encouraging for Claire because she had a tendency to focus on what she had not achieved rather than what she had. Claire then went on to discuss her drive to exercise, in order to prevent her body from changing too much and her need always to eat less than other people. Although she recognised that her preoccupation with food was reducing as she became more flexible about her diet, she felt even more preoccupied with her body than ever, not least because of anxiety about her weight gain. The therapist asked Claire about possible maintaining behaviours, and this revealed a number of rituals that she was engaging in to try to reassure herself that her body was not changing, such as scrutinising herself in the mirror every morning and every night, and trying on the same pair of jeans every day to check that she could still fit into them. The interview also revealed that while school seemed to be going OK, she was getting into lots of arguments at home, leading to guilt and reinforcing her desire to lose weight.

The therapist had asked Claire to fill in and return some questionnaires for homework, so that they could be analysed prior to the review session. These generally showed improvements, apart from the Body Dissatisfaction, Drive for Thinness and Perfectionism subscales of the Eating Disorders Inventory (EDI) and the Family Assessment Device

(FAD), which showed that scores had stayed above the norms across all of the subscales.

Based on the collective findings from the review, Claire and her therapist reviewed the initial formulation (Figure 8.2).

Firstly, the therapist commended Claire on her motivation and commitment to the treatment programme and the positive changes that she had been able to make so far. It was stressed that work on Claire's eating behaviour needed to continue throughout treatment in conjunction with the dietitian and would involve introducing more scary foods and breaking rules about eating. The therapist also explained that in the next few weeks, they would be exploring why shape and weight were so important to Claire as well as exploring whether her need for very high standards was having any negative effect. Claire's need to reassure herself was discussed as something that, on the one hand, had arisen from strict rules regarding her eating and shape but, on the other hand, was perpetuating the rules and often resulted in her being more dissatisfied than satisfied with her body. The results of the FAD were discussed in relation to negative comments about family tension in her diary. The

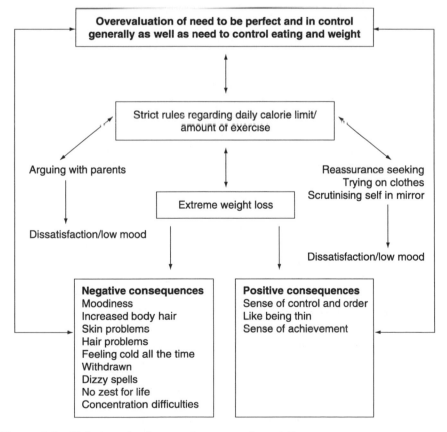

Figure 8.2   Claire's revised anorexia nervosa formulation

therapist acknowledged that while some family tension may be expected, not least because Claire's parents had been encouraged to take a more active role in her eating, this may not be the only reason for any difficulties, and, in any case, they seemed to be having a negative effect on recovery and perhaps warranted further discussion. Claire seemed a little defensive at the suggestion that there may be problems within the family but agreed to explore this with the therapist in future sessions. Lastly, Claire's tendency to focus on the negatives and ignore the positives was noted, and it was agreed that this would be addressed later in the treatment.

Another example

Jake is a 14-year-old boy with AN. Having completed 12 weeks of treatment, he had made some good progress with his eating and was steadily gaining weight. The therapist knew from the sessions and the diary that Jake was eating in a structured way at all times and that he was introducing new foods on a weekly basis. The ratings from the semi-structured interview showed that Jake was able to recognise the changes that had occurred; however, these showed that there were still difficulties around his preoccupation with eating and his rules about it. The interview revealed that although Jake's eating was indeed more flexible in terms of the amounts and types of food eaten, he was spending a long time each evening carefully planning what he was going to eat the next day and went to great lengths to make sure that he stuck to his plan, which was preoccupying him more than ever and in turn made him feel stressed because he couldn't concentrate as well on his schoolwork. Jake was unable to cope with any last-minute changes to his eating plan, such as a spontaneous offer to go out for lunch with friends. This was making him even more stressed and miserable, as he felt like he was missing out on lots of social activities and he worried that people were starting to think that he was odd. Jake scored highly on the Perfectionism subscale of the EDI and despite an initial improvement in his mood, which seemed to coincide with Jake's gaining weight, the Recent Mood and Feelings Questionnaire (MFQ) suggested that Jake's mood was as low as it had been at assessment. Jake's parents gave some feedback about Jake at home, which revealed that he was spending hours in his bedroom during the evenings and weekends doing homework and revision, and that while his teachers were always impressed with how hardworking and bright Jake was, even they had suggested that he may be pushing himself too far.

The therapist summarised the review findings with Jake in the following session and expanded the formulation to take into account the vicious circles he had found himself in. The revised formulation showed that in addition to overvaluing the importance of controlling his eating, Jake was overvaluing the need to be in control – and, indeed, 'perfect' generally and particularly in his schoolwork and at sport (see Figure 8.3).

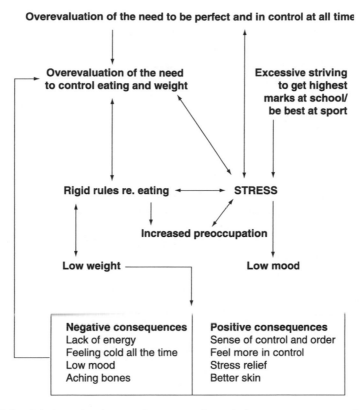

Figure 8.3   Jake's revised anorexia nervosa formulation

This was causing him a great deal of stress, which affected his eating and his mood. Jake recognised this himself but felt that it was such an integral part of his personality that he could not change it; moreover, he was unsure whether he wanted to change it. The therapist assured Jake that she did not want him to change his personality and acknowledged that being in control and having high standards had served him well in the main. She asked Jake whether he thought his life would be better or worse if he had a different view on 'being in control' (for example, being able to make spontaneous decisions about food without feeling anxious), and whether being 'good enough' sometimes rather than perfect all the time would be acceptable. Jake was unsure, but agreed that this needed addressing and was willing to give it a try.

Case example 3

Fiona's initial formulation focused on her overt difficulties with overevaluation of shape and weight (based on a belief that this would make her more likeable), her dieting behaviour and her bingeing and vomiting as well as her low mood. During the first few weeks of treatment, it became apparent that a number of additional factors were contributing to Fiona's eating disorder, and these were explored at the 6-week review and incorporated into her formulation. Of particular significance seemed to be Fiona's highly critical view of herself and her belief that she was not as 'good' as her friends or that if people got to know the 'real' her they would dislike her. As a result, Fiona was drinking a lot of alcohol because she felt that this gave her some confidence. In the longer term, this was having a negative effect on her relationships, which in turn was making her attach even more significance to her belief that if she looked a certain way, people would like her more. This additional information was incorporated into her formulation (Figure 8.4).

Fiona found the review process a little upsetting and felt that her need to lose weight and be the life and soul of the party in order to be liked was 'shallow' and 'weak'. The therapist reframed these thoughts as reflecting a low self-esteem that encouraged a negative, self-critical style of thinking, and it was agreed that this would be addressed later in treatment.

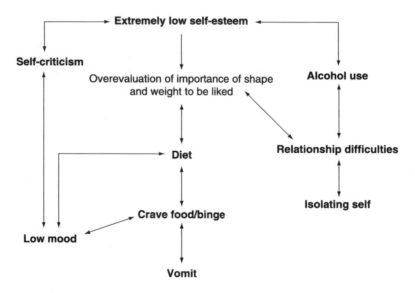

Figure 8.4   Fiona's revised bulimia nervosa formulation

The review process should be collaborative and end with a reformulation of the child's difficulties and a tailor-made action plan

9

Stage 4: addressing unhelpful cognitions and solving problems maintaining the eating disorder

Studies have suggested that negative expectations and attributional style, along with other cognitive distortions and deficits in problem-solving skills, are likely to play an important role in the development and maintenance of emotional and behavioural difficulties in young people. As children develop in a social context, these affect regulation capacities are affected by a variety of factors, and CBT acknowledges that beliefs about shape and weight and their control need to be addressed within this social context. Because children and adolescents may struggle to use deductive reasoning to evaluate the functionality of their beliefs and have a tendency to think in an egocentric manner, cognitive therapy alone is likely to be of limited effectiveness in the majority of cases, and the need for well-designed cognitive behavioural techniques is warranted. There is a growing body of evidence that CBT techniques can bring about change in behavioural and emotional difficulties in young people (Graham, 2005). However, as the evidence for such approaches in young people with eating disorders is in its infancy, some extrapolation from the adult literature is necessary, with some consideration of developmental principles to guide choice and method of intervention. For a comprehensive account of how to use cognitive behavioural techniques with children and young people, readers are directed to Stallard (2002).

Automatic thoughts, dysfunctional attitudes, schemata and behaviour

Automatic thoughts are not peculiar to people with psychological distress – we all experience them, even though we are barely aware of them. Usually, we are more aware of the emotion that accompanies the thought, and this is typically the case for younger people (although, sometimes, they struggle to articulate the emotion). For example, after reading a complicated exam question, a child may have the automatic thought, '*I don't understand it*' but may be more aware of the feeling of panic. Automatic thoughts can be evaluated in terms of their *validity* and *utility*. Whereas some automatic thoughts are distorted in some way, despite objective, contrary evidence, others are accurate but the conclusion drawn from them is not – for example, '*I don't understand the question*' may be an accurate thought, but the conclusion '*therefore I am a stupid person*' is not. Other automatic thoughts may be accurate but unhelpful; for example, '*This homework is really difficult – I'm going to be up for hours if I am to finish it*', may be accurate but is likely to increase anxiety.

The description of negative automatic thoughts (NATS) provided by Beck and colleagues (e.g. Beck *et al.*, 1985) suggests that they are rapid self-statements that can occur in verbal or imaginal form, requiring little conscious processing (although they are amenable to consciousness). They tend to be triggered by events that are either external (e.g. criticism from another person) or internal (e.g. a mood state). While they may be far-fetched and arise despite evidence to the contrary, they often seem highly plausible and reasonable to the subject, and this can make them resistant to change.

> **Negative automatic thoughts are unhelpful and dysfunctional**

Dysfunctional attitudes are usually generalised 'rules for living' that are overly rigid and involve concepts such as 'always', 'never', 'must' and so on. They tend to focus on achievement, approval and/or control, and all three are often present in eating disorders. Dysfunctional attitudes are usually linked to basic hopes about the future (e.g. '*if I get thin, I will be happy*') and are dysfunctional because they prevent people from achieving their goals (e.g. goals regarding thinness are usually shifted, making targets unrealistic and ever changing, and perpetuating the eating disorder and feelings of unhappiness).

> **Dysfunctional attitudes are the unhelpful and unrealistic rules that govern behaviour**

Self–other schemata are built up from experiences we have with significant other people and represent basic core belief structures. They may be difficult to verbalise but are usually experienced as feeling states, as is typically the case for young people. Imagine the following scenario: Dominic, aged 4, runs in a race at his first school fun day and finishes fifth out of 10 class-mates. He dashes over to his dad proudly with a big smile, only to be told: 'Never mind – try to win the next one instead.' Not only is Dominic likely to experience his father as being disappointed in him, but he is also likely to see himself as a failure, leading to feelings of guilt and shame. Such repeated experience throughout a child's life can have a disastrous effect on his internal experiences, leading to the development of a negative schema (e.g. 'I am unworthy and a failure'). Consider a more positive response: Dad picks Dominic up and tells him how well he did and what a great runner he is. Not only does Dominic experience his father as proud, but he also has positive emotions in *himself about himself*, increasing the likelihood that he will develop a positive schema: 'I am worthy, able and competent.'

> Positive and negative core beliefs and schemata are developed from important experiences in childhood

NATS, assumptions about life and schemata ultimately lead to social behaviour; thus, when working with young people with eating disorders, it is important for the therapist to understand these cognitive processes and to include them when formulating difficulties. However, this can be challenging, not least because of patients' tendency to conceal, compensate for, or avoid triggering core negative beliefs through their actions. Consider the following examples:

- A core belief that 'I am a failure' may lead to overcompensation by overworking or complete avoidance – not bothering to try.
- A core belief that others will reject me if I upset them may lead to anger inhibition or lack of assertiveness.

Young's schema-focused model (Young, 1999) has been used successfully in treating patients with a range of disorders; indeed, Waller *et al.* (2007a) have described schema-focused CBT (SFCBT) for use with adults with eating disorders. This attempts to modify beliefs that create unacceptable emotions. In our experience, SFCBT can be helpful for older (but not necessarily younger) children, and the reader is directed to Waller *et al.* (2007b) for a more comprehensive account of this approach.

In addition to using the diary to illuminate the link between thoughts, feelings and behaviour, therapists should be alert to their own observations of interactions within sessions and feed these back to the patient. Because such observations are instant and tangible, they tend to make some sense to even very young patients. Usually, reports from other family members are useful in providing some insight into the patient's thinking style, and working with the family together, including siblings, can be especially revealing.

Ultimately, patients need to be able to increase their own self-awareness in order to develop more helpful cognitive and behavioural skills and move to a more functional cycle. It is the therapist's role to teach patients how to do this, by modelling the process during sessions and asking probing questions. For example:

'What was the first thought that came into your mind when I just told you that I would be weighing you at every session?'

'How did it make you feel?'

What do you think the consequence of my weighing you will be?

The vicious cycle can then be clearly explained to patients, as in Figure 9.1.

Negative thinking styles

Negative thinking styles reflect a bias in interpretation that is consistent with NATS and dysfunctional attitudes. Some of the most common ones are described below:

- **Dichotomous thinking:** seeing something in only two categories rather than on a continuum: *'If I am not thin, I must be fat.'*
- **Catastrophising:** focusing on the worst possible outcome of a situation and overestimating the likelihood that it will occur: *'If I eat a biscuit, I will lose control and be unable to stop bingeing for the rest of the day.'*
- **Magnification/minimisation:** enlarging the importance of negative experiences or weaknesses and discounting the importance of the positives or forgetting strengths: *'It doesn't matter that I didn't binge in the week because I ruined everything by bingeing at the weekend.'*
- **Personalising failures:** directly relating negative events to the self when there is no obvious reason to do so: *'It is my fault that my parents have split up.'*
- **Mental filtering:** focusing on one (negative) aspect of a situation rather than looking at the whole picture: *'My best friend is smaller than me' (ignoring the fact that most people in the class are either similar to or bigger than me).*
- **Mind reading:** assuming that others are reacting negatively to you when there is no direct evidence for this: *'I know everyone thinks I look fat.'*
- **Double standards:** having more stringent standards for the self than for others: *'It's OK for everyone else to eat puddings but it's not OK for me.'*
- **Emotional reasoning:** feeling something makes it true: *'I feel fat; therefore, I am.'*

Negative thinking styles are biases in cognitive processing that help to maintain the eating disorder

---

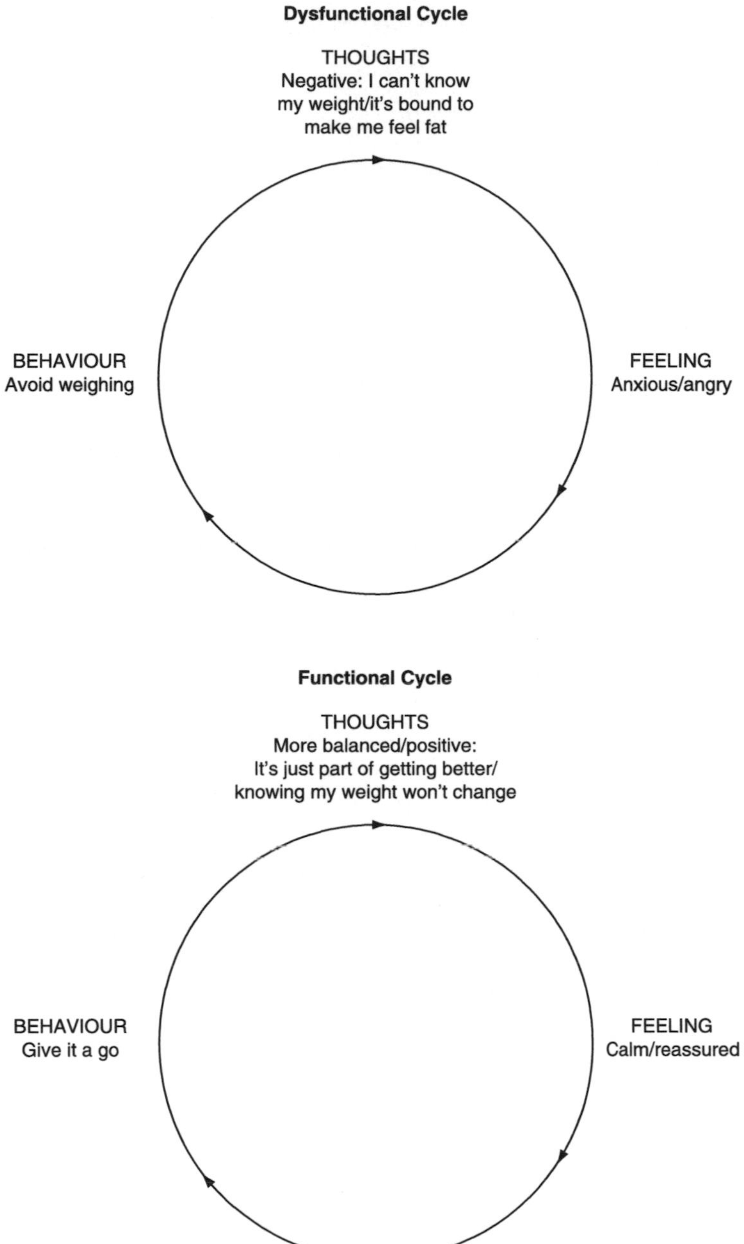

Dysfunctional Cycle

THOUGHTS
Negative: I can't know
my weight/it's bound to
make me feel fat

BEHAVIOUR
Avoid weighing

FEELING
Anxious/angry

Functional Cycle

THOUGHTS
More balanced/positive:
It's just part of getting better/
knowing my weight won't change

BEHAVIOUR
Give it a go

FEELING
Calm/reassured

Figure 9.1 Functional and dysfunctional cycles

Useful techniques for addressing unhelpful thinking styles and related thoughts

Downward arrow technique

This is a useful technique to help patients to 'decatastrophise' and challenge the black and white thinking common in those with eating disorders. It involves asking patients what personal meaning their thoughts have to them, and it often results in the identification of core beliefs.

> *Jake's concern about becoming stocky had led him to overexercise and push himself too hard during football training, and this was not only contributing to his weight loss but was also making him increasingly rundown and tired, and he was having to miss football games because of illness and injuries. His therapist suggested that he reduce the number of times he trained per week, but he reacted badly to this.*

Therapist: Jake, you seem to be reacting badly to the suggestion that you reduce the number of times you train – what are your concerns about this?

Jake: I would lose my fitness.

Therapist: And what would the implications of that be?

Jake: All my hard work would have been for nothing.

Therapist: How would that be?

Jake: I would get dropped from the team for sure.

Therapist: And assuming that were true, what would the consequences be?

Jake: My friends wouldn't want to know me and my dad would be really disappointed in me.

Therapist: And how do you think that would that make you feel?

Jake: Like I've let everybody down.

Therapist: Anything else?

Jake: Depressed and like a complete failure.

Therapist: So all this would happen because you reduced (not stopped) your training sessions?

Jake: Well, I suppose, when you put it like that, it's probably quite unlikely . . .

Therapist: Yes, maybe it is, but can you see how your chain of negative thoughts leads you to assume that catastrophe would result from reducing your training sessions?

Jake: Yes, I suppose it does seem a bit dramatic.

> *The therapist and the patient can then illustrate what has been learnt by summarising the points on paper, as below:*

Automatic thought = 'I cannot reduce my training'
↓
I would lose my fitness
↓
I would get dropped from the team
↓
I would lose my friends
↓
My dad would be disappointed
↓
I would let everybody down
↓
Underlying belief = **I would be a failure**

This exercise not only helped Jake to articulate his fears but also enabled him to see for himself the distortion in his thinking and specifically his tendency to catastrophise. Through further discussion, he was able to see that, ironically, he would be much more likely to feel like a failure if he carried on with his intense training regime because it was having such an adverse effect on his health, his social life, his football and even his school work.

Monitoring

Once patients are aware of the existence of their unhelpful thinking styles, the next step is to help increase their awareness of the extent of them, by paying particular attention to them through prescribed monitoring. So as not to overload the young person, the therapist and patient should pick something specific to focus on, such as 'black and white thinking', and the patient should practise spotting when this occurs as a homework task. Separate record sheets can be devised for this exercise; however, we prefer to continue with the existing diary to record this information, partly because it seems more manageable for the young person but also because this makes it easier to observe and demonstrate links between the young person's thinking style and eating behaviour. As a further step, and particularly once patients have started to address their unhelpful thinking style, monitoring examples of *not* engaging in this style and the impact that it has is also useful.

Figure 9.2 shows a sample page from Jake's diary identifying his tendency to think in a black and white way.

Drawing attention to the use of words such as 'never' and 'every' is helpful in enabling children to identify this phenomenon, and, while initially, this recognition may be retrospective, in time, they should be able to catch themselves engaging in this type of thinking.

Evaluating evidence

Once patients understand their biased and unhelpful cognitions, considering the evidence for and against them is helpful. However, this is often

Date: 7.2.08 (Thurs)				
H/wk task: Real time recording				
Time	Place	Food consumed	Compensatory behaviours	What am I thinking/feeling/doing?
7.20	Kitchen	Bowl of branflakes + ss milk/1 x toast + marg + glass of OJ		Tired. Not too hungry this morning.
7.50			Went for 40-min. run	If I don't go running every morning I'll get fat and lazy.
11.00	School	Banana		Am quite hungry but don't want to eat too much.
12.30	Canteen	2 ham butties + Special K bar + low-fat yogurt		Could never eat a 'normal' yogurt like dietitian suggested – far too much fat.
4.15	Footy ground	1 bottle of Lucozade		At footy training – my friends are all fitter than me – they always get praise from the coach. Having drink to give me more energy.
6.30	Kitchen	Fish, jacket potato + salad + low-fat rice pudding + chocolate digestive	Sit-ups straight after tea	Got tummyache – should've waited before exercising. Feel awful about chocolate biscuit – I am never going to get better at this rate.
9.30	Bedroom			Bed – no supper. 😊

Figure 9.2   Jake's diary page

surprisingly difficult for youngsters to do, and this difficulty is exacerbated by the presence of one or more unhelpful cognitive styles, such as a tendency to minimise positives and apply mental filters. For example, if asked to record evidence for and against the belief 'other people think I am unattractive', it would not be uncommon for the child to come back with a long list of points under 'evidence for' and nothing under 'evidence against'. Rather than this reflecting an unwillingness to complete the exercise, it is more likely to be a result of *not seeing* the evidence. The therapist may therefore need to spend some time teaching the patient how to spot the evidence (for example, by modelling this in the session) and address any additional impeding thinking styles.

Continua/orthogonal lines

The use of continua to address black and white thinking is well documented, and, as mentioned elsewhere in this book, such thinking is common not only in eating disorders but also among children and teenagers in general. For those with AN in particular, polarised views about fatness and thinness are typical, and encouraging patients to view weight/shape on a continuum can be challenging. While in an ideal world, patients would not be valuing or striving for thinness at all, it can be helpful and more realistic to look for a compromise towards acceptance of 'slim-normal' rather than 'the thinnest'. Using continuum lines in conjunction with BMI percentiles is useful here. For example, at the start of treatment, Emma believed that her current weight of 46 kg made her fat and strived to be a 'slim' 40 kg, as shown in Figure 9.3.

The therapist used the BMI percentile chart for girls (see Chapter 3) to show an objective picture of thinness and fatness, and plotted Emma's current BMI, which was around the 0.4th percentile, as well as her desired BMI, which was off the scale altogether. This led on to a discussion about how realistic Emma's desire to be 40 kg was and how helpful it was.

The therapist used this information to encourage Emma to accept a more realistic target weight at around the 25th percentile, which, as demonstrated by the continuum line, was still a long way from being fat (Figure 9.4).

Continuum lines are a useful way of challenging dichotomous thinking

---

While continuum lines such as these can be extremely useful when working with this type of thinking error, sometimes, black and white thinking can be extremely personalised and linked to core beliefs and may involve two or more interacting beliefs.

> *For example, Fiona had low self-esteem as well as a tendency to dichotomous thinking, which exacerbated her eating difficulties. During the sessions, her therapist helped her to uncover a range of dichotomous beliefs about her attractiveness and happiness; however, to complicate*

Figure 9.3   Emma's dichotomous view of weight

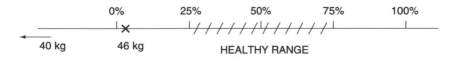

Figure 9.4   A balanced view of weight

matters, these beliefs were intrinsically linked to being thin: for example, 'If I am thin I will be popular/attractive.'

While Fiona had never been 100 per cent confident about her weight and appearance, her dissatisfaction had increased following the break-up with her boyfriend a year before, prompting her to go on a diet. Initially, she did feel better after losing some weight, but she soon started to feel emotionally drained, irritable and unable to concentrate on her school-work. Gradually, she fell into an unhelpful pattern of restricting, bingeing and vomiting, which resulted in her regaining some of the lost weight and feeling even worse than she had prior to losing weight. She believed that if she could just get back to restricting her eating and lose a bit more weight, she would feel good about herself. Although Fiona had made some progress in regulating her eating and reintroducing some avoided foods, her cognitions about being thin were preventing her from implementing the strategies on a consistent basis, and this was keeping her in a vicious eating disorder cycle.

The therapist asked Fiona to pick one belief about being thin, and she chose, 'The thinner I am, the more popular I will be.' Next, the therapist asked Fiona to write down the names of as many people as she could think of in her school year, including her own circle of friends as well as groups she did not mix much with. Fiona enjoyed telling her therapist about the different groups within her year and gave them all names, such as 'the goths', 'the bookworms' and 'the emos'. Once the list had been compiled, two separate headings were added, one for 'thinness' and one for 'popularity'. As a homework task, Fiona was to rate the individuals according to how thin and how popular they were on a scale of 0–10, 10 being the thinnest and most popular. It is important that patients be happy with the accuracy of their ratings before progressing to the next stage to minimise any tendency to disregard the findings. In the following session, the therapist presented Fiona with a blank graph and asked her to plot her scores, which looked something like Figure 9.5.

Once the graph was complete, the therapist asked Fiona whether she could draw any conclusions from it. Even if the conclusions seem obvious, it is crucial that the patient, and not the therapist, identify these, not least because the patient's biased thinking may result in misinterpreting information or downplaying certain aspects. In our experience, this exercise always results in a random scattering, as opposed to the linear association that the patient may have been expecting. It is helpful for the therapist to draw such a linear association on the graph (see Figure 9.6) to demonstrate that many people fall outside the diagonal line, and to use this information to help question whether the belief that thinness = popular is true.

The therapist and Fiona then spent the remainder of the session discussing the findings from the graph in more detail. They acknowledged that there were more people in the top right-hand corner of the graph, suggesting that there were slightly more people on the thin side of normal and more popular than unpopular ones within her year group. This did

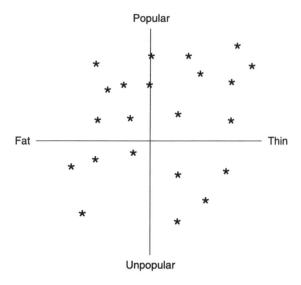

Figure 9.5   Orthogonal lines of fatness and popularity

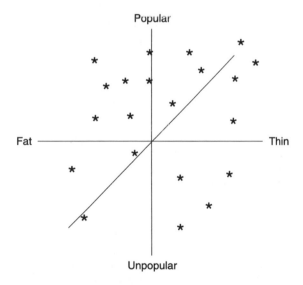

Figure 9.6   Orthogonal lines of fatness and popularity with 'expected' association

not, however, necessarily mean that the thinner you are the more popular you are, as some of the thinnest people were also the most unpopular and some of the fattest people were extremely popular. As a homework task, Fiona went through all of the people who scored highly on popularity and identified additional factors, other than weight, which contributed to their popularity. As is always the case when working towards modifying beliefs, it is important to retain a 'curious' stance during this exercise rather than give patients the impression that you want to disprove their beliefs, or that you already know what the findings will be.

> Orthogonal lines provide an objective way of comparing the predicted relationship between two characteristics

Behavioural experiments

Behavioural experiments are used to test the validity of patients' eating disorder-related beliefs and core beliefs and to test alternative, more adaptive perspectives. They are extremely powerful because they provide hard evidence directly related to the belief(s) and as such promote greater cognitive, emotional and behavioural change than verbal cognitive techniques used in isolation. They therefore reduce the likelihood of patients saying, 'I can understand it logically but I still don't feel it' – a common frustration for people with eating disorders. It is important that alternative beliefs as well as current beliefs be identified prior to the actual experiment, and therefore experiments do require careful prior planning. However, subsequent experiments may happen 'accidentally' and can also be helpful in contributing to disconfirmation of old beliefs and generation of new ones. While carrying out the experiment, it is important that patients maintain some consistency in other aspects of their behaviour, to avoid any 'extraneous variance' and the likelihood that any findings will be disregarded or seen as atypical.

> *Fiona never ate in restaurants, with either her friends or her family, as she believed that this would result in a binge followed by vomiting and thus keep her bulimic cycle going. Fiona and her friends were all in sixth form together, and eating out, at either McDonald's or sandwich bars at lunchtime or for evening meals was a regular occurrence among the group. The therapist believed that her avoidance was a significant maintaining factor for her eating disorder, for several reasons. For example, Fiona would go for long periods of time without eating rather than eat with others, and this increased the likelihood of bingeing later on; and her feeling increasingly left out when friends were enjoying meals out together was affecting her mood, and in turn increasing her tendency to binge. Fiona felt that this was something she wanted to tackle in treatment, even though she was filled with anxiety at the thought of eating with others.*
>
> *Firstly, Fiona's current thought or 'target cognition' was identified:* 'If I go for a meal in a restaurant it will lead to a binge followed by vomiting; therefore, I must avoid this at all costs.' *She predicted that her friends would be so surprised if she ate with them, that they would draw attention to it, increasing her anxiety and making her even more likely to lose control. Fiona was encouraged to generate an alternative perspective:* 'If I stop avoiding this, I will become less isolated from my friends, which will make me feel happier and less likely to binge.'
>
> *Then, Fiona and her therapist decided to devise an experiment to test her beliefs, and it was agreed that the next time her friends were*

eating out she would join them. She was asked to record how she felt before and immediately after the experiment as well as to pay attention to her friends' reaction during the experiment.

Results and reflection.

Fiona had an opportunity to carry out the experiment a couple of days later, when her friends were going to McDonald's for lunch. Although she rated her anxiety levels as being particularly high prior to the experiment, she was able to go through with it, and she chose a salad, which she was able to eat without going on to binge and vomit. She was surprised that her friends did not comment on the fact that she was joining them and reflected that after the meal she felt relieved and pleased with herself. However, although Fiona felt that the experiment had been partially successful in challenging her belief that eating out would lead to vomiting, she downplayed her success a little by attributing this to the fact that she chose only a salad.

This was addressed in a couple of ways. Firstly, the therapist reminded Fiona of her tendency to minimise any positives and shift goalposts, and encouraged her to consider whether she was doing this here (after all, the negative belief was about eating out per se, not about specific foods). Secondly, the therapist suggested that Fiona continue to test the validity of her old and new beliefs by looking for further opportunities to carry out experiments, using a hierarchy of fearful situations. This generally results in patients becoming more confident in taking risks and therefore speeds up the process of generating more helpful beliefs and predictions.

> Behavioural experiments provide powerful and objective ways of testing cognitions

Surveys

A survey is a type of behavioural experiment used to generate evidence to challenge unhelpful beliefs by using feedback from other people. Surveys are therefore particularly helpful if the belief is related to others; for example, 'Other people think I look fat' (an example of mind-reading). In conducting a survey, attention should be paid to the following:

- Any questions should be devised beforehand with the patient.
- Consideration should be given to the question of who should be targeted in the survey.
- The patient's expectations should be elicited prior to conducting the survey.

Fiona believed that she looked fat to others, despite having a healthy BMI of 19.5, and this belief was interfering with her recovery. She disregarded comments from friends and family that she was attractive, because she felt that they were biased and just wanted to make her feel good, so her therapist suggested that they try to gather some evidence to help confirm or disconfirm her belief in a way that would be meaningful to Fiona. The idea of presenting a photograph of Fiona to strangers and asking for, and tape-recording, their opinion was presented to her, and although she was extremely anxious about this and convinced herself that it would just confirm her belief that people thought she was fat, Fiona was willing to give it a try. She did not want to carry out the survey herself, as she thought this would be too embarrassing, but she agreed to bring in two photographs of herself, one of her wearing casual, everyday clothes and one of her dressed for going out, for her therapist to use. Initially, Fiona was sceptical and felt that the therapist would tell the respondents what to say or delete any negative comment. So the therapist had to agree not to do either of these things, and, in turn, Fiona had to agree to trust that the therapist would not do this (otherwise, there would be no point in conducting the survey). Next, Fiona and her therapist discussed what questions would be asked in the survey and agreed the following:

- *What are your first impressions of this girl based on these two photographs?*
- *What are your views on her shape?*
- *How attractive or unattractive do you think she is?*

While it was crucial that the questions reflected what Fiona wanted to find out, it was important that the questions were not worded too negatively (e.g. 'Do you think she looks fat and ugly'?), not least because this could make respondents feel uncomfortable and affect their response but also because this could reinforce Fiona's negative view of herself. It was agreed that the therapist would target a range of people, both male and female, of varying ages. Sometimes, patients are specific about whose views they are interested in, such as just females of a similar age, and it was therefore important that the therapist consider how feasible it is to access a particular group before setting up the exercise. Lastly, Fiona's expected and alternative beliefs were identified.

Expected beliefs

- *Other people will describe me as fat/chubby and unattractive.*
- *They will comment on my large thighs and round face.*

Alternative beliefs

- *Other people will not describe my appearance in negative terms (as indicated by the absence of negative comments, neutral comments or positive comments).*

- *Other people may see me differently (e.g. more positively) from the way that I see myself.*

The therapist carried out the survey as agreed, and in a subsequent session, she played the tape recording of the various comments to Fiona. In our experience, this kind of exercise always results in the expected beliefs being disconfirmed, and this was the case here. Fiona was surprised not only at the absence of critical comments about her appearance but also at the numerous positive comments that people made; for example, regarding her pretty face. She was also surprised to hear people comment on other aspects of her appearance, such as her nice dress sense and shiny hair, which she herself tended to ignore because she was too busy focusing on the bits of herself that she disliked, such as her legs and round face. The exercise enabled Fiona to begin considering the alternative view that other people might see her more positively than how she saw herself, and provided a useful starting point for further work on her body image.

> **Surveys provide a way of challenging mind-reading distortions**

Positive data logs

Used widely in the depression field, positive data logs enable patients to become more conscious of the positive things they may be overlooking, thereby helping them to come to a more balanced decision about whether their negative beliefs are accurate or not. For example, a patient who believes that everyone thinks she is unattractive may be asked to look out for and record in the diary any examples of positive comments or situations, however minor, which do not fit in with this belief, such as recording compliments. Some children find this especially challenging, particularly those with very low self-esteem or with highly rigid beliefs. In such cases, it can be helpful to ask the child to practise recording positives in relation to more neutral areas before progressing to more sensitive ones.

> **Positive data logs provide a way of challenging strong negative core beliefs and schemata**

Imagery

Imagery techniques can be extremely powerful in helping patients to challenge negative thoughts and distract from urges or cravings. Examples of imagery include imagining saying 'no' in an assertive but polite way

Table 9.1 Matching problematic thinking to cognitive techniques

	Downward arrowing	Monitoring	Surveys	Behavioural experiments	Positive data logs	Continual/ orthogonal lines	Evaluating evidence
Dichotomous thinking	*	*		*		*	*
Catastrophising	*	*				*	*
Magnification/minimisation	*	*	*		*		*
Personalising failures	*	*	*		*		*
Mental filtering		*		*			*
Mind-reading		*		*	*	*	*
Double standards	*	*		*			*
Emotional reasoning		*		*	*		*

to a second helping of chocolate cake, to avoid a binge episode; imagining being happy, sociable and enjoying life as a result of being able to eat out with friends; and imagining alternatives to specific eating disordered behaviours at mealtimes. When used to challenge negative/core beliefs, imagery can have quite a dramatic effect. For example, in cases where bullying or teasing has been present, patients are asked to imagine the scenario as vividly as possible, paying attention to macrodetails such as time of day, what people were wearing and so on, as well as focusing on thoughts and feelings associated with the scenario. They are then asked to respond to the scenario with a newer, healthy response. For example, this may involve walking away from the bullies or challenging them, the aim being to create distance from the scenario and ultimately the beliefs that have arisen as a result. We find that although this technique works less well with younger children (because they either may find the task embarrassing or get easily distracted from completing the process), it can be extremely valuable for older or more mature children and is therefore worth considering.

> Imagery can provide a useful way of helping children plan how to deal with difficult situations or consider different outcomes

Most of the techniques described here can be adapted for use with any of the problematic thinking styles; however, Table 9.1 suggests which particular set of techniques may be most suited to a particular thinking style.

Problem solving

Many patients with eating disorders have deficits in problem solving, and this can exacerbate tendencies to binge, cut back on eating, or engage in other compensatory behaviours. Learning effective problem-solving skills can not only help patients to control their eating behaviour but should also improve their ability to cope with general difficulties in life, both during and beyond treatment. There are variations on how to teach and employ problem-solving techniques, but, essentially, the following six steps underpin the procedure:

Step 1: identify the problem. It is crucial that problems be defined clearly and specifically, rather than being vague and generalised accounts of ongoing difficulties. For example, identifying 'feeling down' as a problem that can trigger problematic eating may well be true; however, such a vague description is unlikely to result in helpful solutions being generated, whereas 'feeling down because I am anxious about my exams next week' is much more specific.

Step 2: *identify potential solutions.* A dichotomous thinking style is present in many patients with eating disorders, resulting in a tendency to offer polar opposite solutions to problems ('*I can either avoid the cake altogether or eat the whole lot*') with little thought to all the options between. The therapist should encourage patients to identify as many potential solutions as possible to the problem they have identified, even if they seem unrealistic to them at first, to encourage more flexible thought and eventually lead to new options being considered. While it is preferable that the potential solutions be generated by the patient, the therapist may need to prompt and in some cases offer some suggestions, rather like a brainstorming exercise. This is particularly the case in the early stages of teaching problem solving and with younger patients; however, once patients are well practised, they should be able to generate their own solutions without the help of the therapist.

Step 3: *think through the implications of each solution.* Once all the potential solutions have been identified, the therapist should ask the patient to imagine carrying out each solution and think about what the impact of it might be. This may be a relatively easy task, especially if the patient has tried that particular solution before; however, for younger patients in particular, thinking through the implications of new solutions can be a tricky and time-consuming exercise. It is, however, an important one and should not be rushed. If therapists feel that patients are not thinking through the solutions carefully enough, they should ask questions to encourage them to do so. For example, a young person may offer a solution of having a bath to relax in order to avoid feeling stressed and anxious after having her evening meal. While this may seem like a reasonable solution, the therapist may know from the patient's diary that having a bath when feeling bloated increases the likelihood that she will scrutinise her body, an act that typically leads to dissatisfaction and ultimately problematic behaviour. Socratic questioning should be used to help the patient to see this for herself.

Step 4: *choose a solution.* This is usually the most straightforward aspect of problem solving because if the previous steps have been followed correctly, it tends to be fairly obvious which solution makes most sense – or at least which solutions *do not* seem realistic. In some cases, it may be useful to combine more than one solution, and patients should be encouraged to do this if appropriate. Unless the chosen solution seems wholly inappropriate, the therapist should resist the urge to change the patient's mind – an alternative solution can always be tried at a later date. Although 'allowing' a patient to go through with a solution that the therapist is sure will be ineffective may seem like a waste of time, it is important that to some degree, the patient learn from her own mistakes and take some responsibility for decision making. This will increase self-efficacy and confidence, whereas telling patients what to do will not.

Step 5: carry out the solution. After the solution has been agreed on, it is important to devise a clear plan to enable the patient to put it into practice. Once patients become more confident in problem solving, they are better able to cope with not sticking rigidly to the plan that has been devised but rather taking on board the essence of it, whereas younger patients and those new to problem solving seem to benefit from having clear guidelines to follow.

Step 6: review the process. This final step should not be neglected, regardless of whether the solution worked well or not. It involves reviewing steps 1–5 to see whether they were carried out properly and whether they could have been improved. If the exercise went well, it is useful to acknowledge that – not just in terms of being able to identify a useful coping strategy for a particular problem but also to increase young persons' confidence in their ability to solve problems effectively. This will encourage them to use it again in the future. If the solution was unsuccessful in bringing about positive change, it is crucial to review why this might have been, to avoid feelings of hopelessness ('*Nothing works – I may as well give up*') and encourage a more optimistic and pragmatic approach to overcoming problems.

Difficulties with problem solving

Often, patients who present with eating disorders are intelligent and thoughtful individuals who know what steps they 'should' take to solve their problem, but unhelpful thoughts or cognitive styles may prevent them from implementing them.

> *Fiona, a 17-year-old girl with BN, found that concentrating on revision for her A levels was a problem that inevitably resulted in bingeing. Her solution list, together with the implications, was as follows:*
>
> 1   Take a break and watch television: *Initial relief to get away from books but would get bored and restless watching TV and would probably start to pick at food, which would make me more irritable and more likely to give up and binge.*
> 2   Go to bed: *It's not as if I would be able to switch off and sleep because I would just lie there worrying for ages and feel like a failure and would eventually get up and have a really late binge which would make me feel even worse the next day.*
> 3   Go out for a walk: *It would be good to get out of the house and get some fresh air; however, I would start to panic that I should be at home working. I would probably buy some chocolate from the shop and then end up bingeing.*
> 4   Stay in bedroom and persevere: *I have already tried this loads of times – it is nothing new and just increases my frustration and therefore the likelihood that I will binge.*
> 5   Discuss difficulties with my tutor: *I could do this, but I would not want*

him to think that I am not coping or that I need 'special' help – this would make me feel even worse. There would not be much he could do anyway, as the problem is generally in the evening time.

6   Call a friend: *This may make me feel better in the short term because it would distract me from the work. However, I would feel guilty because I know that they are all busy with their own revision and it wouldn't be fair to distract them.*

7   Download a revision self-help book from the Internet: *This may offer new, practical solutions that I have not tried before – could be worth a try.*

Fiona chose solution 7, as she felt that this could not only help her to revise better but also prevent her from bingeing. Having devised and implemented the solution, she reflected that it had been partially successful in that she did learn new techniques that helped with the revision process. However, she still had some difficulty in concentrating, particularly with subjects that she struggled with, and although her bingeing was delayed, it still happened at the end of the evening.

Fiona and her therapist reviewed the process of problem solving in the following session. Both agreed that the problem had been accurately defined and that she had come up with a good selection of potential solutions. Given that the chosen solution had been partially successful, it seemed a reasonable choice; however, it was possible that other potentially helpful solutions had been either missed or wrongly rejected. Fiona went through her list of solutions and immediately dismissed 1–4 as being unhelpful and almost certainly unlikely to solve the problem and prevent bingeing. This left 'discussing her difficulties with her tutor' and 'calling a friend'. It was clear that Fiona was uneasy about both of these options, despite knowing that they made some sense and would appeal to others in her position. The therapist suspected that Fiona's low self-esteem and related beliefs may have been underpinning her reluctance, and he used Socratic questioning and downward arrowing to stimulate Fiona's awareness of this and uncover some fundamental negative beliefs, such as, 'If others see me not coping, they will think negatively of me.' The therapist referred to the formulation that they had recently revised, indicating that Fiona had very low self-esteem, manifested in beliefs that she did not deserve attention and support from others and that if others saw the 'real her' they would not want to know her. Fiona was able to see that her low self-esteem and related belief systems were probably preventing her from implementing potentially helpful solutions to her difficulties; although frustrating, this made her more determined to tackle the problem during treatment.

A key step in problem solving is reflecting on the process and outcome

Dealing with body image and overevaluation of shape and weight

Body image refers to the internal picture we have of our own physical appearance and is based not only on what we see in the mirror but also, largely, on how we feel. Young people with eating disorders often have an unrealistic body image, in that they see themselves as 'too fat' even though they are at a normal or low weight. Sometimes, patients tell us that they *know* they are too thin or have an unrealistic body image, and while one might expect treatment in these latter cases to be easier, the challenges remain the same: to help the young person develop a more realistic body image, which tends to involve acceptance of a current or new body shape rather than 100 per cent satisfaction with body shape, which is rarely achieved. In this age group generally, concerns about appearance are common; however, for some of our patients with eating disorders, issues to do with control, particularly in the context of family relationships, may seem more prominent than body concerns per se. In any case, by definition, a fear of fatness or overevaluation of body shape is always present in patients with AN or BN, and at some point in treatment, body image almost universally needs to be addressed. In this section, we will not be discussing body image problems in the obese client group; however, some of the principles may be applied as appropriate in such cases where there is an eating disorder present.

In the adult field, it has been suggested that educating patients about the functions of their body and helping them to understand the role of physiology is a useful adjunct to body image work. However, while parents often find this information useful and are keen for their child to consider such information, we find that this is helpful for only a minority of older teenagers, and so it may be more helpful to give patients a handout to read with an invitation to discuss the issues in more detail either with their therapist or with a specialist dietitian, rather than risking alienating the patient through discussion of these matters in the session.

Understanding the development of the child's self-image is important, as treatment needs to be tailor-made to take into account the beliefs associated with both the development and maintenance of body image disturbance. It might seem reasonable to assume that a grossly abnormal body image is a precipitating factor for the eating disorder, and while this is sometimes the case, we have found that in other cases the initial body image disturbance is relatively mild but becomes much more pronounced as the eating disorder develops. Alternatively, some patients present with a more complex history, involving bullying, teasing or abuse, which has contributed to the development of a negative body image, usually linked to core beliefs about the self and others, and therefore this can be extremely resistant to change. In most cases, we find that it is easier at least to begin addressing difficulties relating to the *maintenance* of *current* body image concerns before exploring the development of those concerns in more detail.

Body image concerns do seem more pronounced during pubescence and in the early stages of adolescence. The onset of puberty causes misgivings in many; indeed, some authorities have viewed the impact of puberty as the chief experiential aetiological issue underlying the development of eating disorders (Crisp, 1994). Some young people do indeed restrict their eating in a conscious attempt to reverse the development of puberty. Some concerns may arise out of unhappiness with specific changes affecting the body during this time, particularly the onset of menstruation in females. Sometimes, this seems to be about discomfort with sexuality in general; sometimes, more about physical discomfort, embarrassment or more general concerns about growing up. A desire to remain 'childlike' can have a number of origins, and issues relating to control (for example, controlling family relationships and in particular parental behaviour) are often central.

Parents' (understandable) concerns can typically lead to overemphasis on the negative effects of delayed puberty, and while it is important to convey these to the child, it needs to be done carefully and sensitively to avoid exacerbating the problem.

Overevaluation of the importance of shape and weight (and controlling eating) is central to the cognitive behavioural perspective of eating disorders (Fairburn *et al.*, 1999; Slade, 1982) and typically is intrinsically linked to self-esteem: '*As long as I am thin, I can feel good about myself.*' While patients are often aware of this belief system, they tend not to be aware of the validity and usefulness of such a system, and this may be particularly the case for younger patients, because of their level of social, emotional and cognitive development.

A helpful way to explore this with patients is to use a self-evaluation pie chart, as described by Fairburn (e.g. Fairburn, 2007). The main aim of the self-evaluation pie chart is to encourage patients to change the way they judge themselves, by increasing their awareness of the unhelpful biases operating within the current system and finding alternative ways of valuing themselves.

> *Emma is a 16-year-old girl with binge-purging anorexia, with aspirations to be a model. She gets on quite well with her mother but has a difficult relationship with her stepfather and tends to compete with him for her mother's attention. Emma feels angry with her biological father for leaving her mum and dislikes his new girlfriend. She has some good friendships. However, her moodiness has started to affect these friendships and her social life. The therapist asked Emma to complete a self-evaluation pie chart, with the question, 'How do you judge yourself as a person?'*

It is important that patients do not complete an 'ideal' pie chart or list the values that they would like to have or think they should have at this stage. For younger patients or those who may be struggling with the concept, asking them when they last felt good or bad about themselves can be a helpful way of encouraging them to think about how they value themselves. As a therapist, it can be useful to model this by completing your own pie chart for the patient first – it does not need to be accurate – you are just modelling the principle.

Emma's initial self-evaluation pie chart looked like Figure 9.7.

Almost three-quarters of Emma's pie chart was taken up by shape and weight, with the remaining four segments being squashed into one-quarter of the chart. She was embarrassed by the chart, as she felt that it made her seem superficial and uncaring. However, the therapist did not focus on this but rather gave lots of positive reinforcement for Emma's honesty.

Some tips for completing the self-evaluation pie chart:

- Do not rush it. If you do not have sufficient time in the session, explain the concept and ask patients to think about it and complete it for home-work, and then review it in the following session.
- Stress that you are not judging the patient.
- Explain that just because shape/weight may take up more space than, for example, relationship with parents, this does not mean that the patient does not care about her mum and dad.
- Stress that while self-evaluation may be resistant to change if it is not addressed, it is not fixed for life and *can* change – as long as patients want it to.

Changing the self-evaluation system

Once patients have completed their self-evaluation pie chart, the focus shifts to learning about its function and deciding whether or not to keep hold of it. Typically, patients are surprised and sometimes saddened to be faced with the reality of their pie chart because they had not realised just how important shape and weight had become to them, relative to other factors in their life. Therapists should demonstrate how the self-evaluation system is perpetuating the eating disorder, by illustrating the following main points:

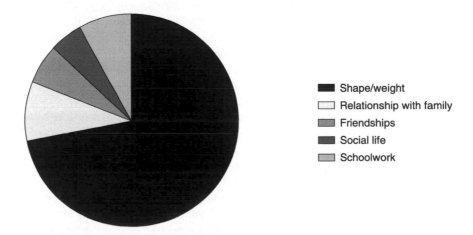

Figure 9.7   Emma's self-evaluation pie chart

1   'Eggs are all in one basket.' Explain that judging yourself almost entirely in one domain results in a lot of pressure to achieve in that particular domain and if anything goes wrong with it, you are likely to feel terrible.
2   Goals are often unachievable. Unachievable or unrealistic goals mean setting yourself up for failure, and this can be a vicious cycle because the more you fail, the harder you strive and so on.
3   The overvalued domains replace other important domains in life. By focusing on one particular domain and seeing life exclusively through that domain, you push out other (more helpful and realistic) potential domains for self-evaluation.

Following a discussion with her therapist, Emma was able to see how unhelpful her system of self-evaluation was. She could see that not only was the importance she attached to shape and weight displacing other important aspects in her life, but that it was directly competing with them. For example, as she had already identified earlier in treatment, she had a range of problems secondary to her eating disorder, including mood swings and social withdrawal, and this was having a negative effect on all of her relationships as well as her social life. She was not even happy with her 'valued' domain of shape and weight because she had recently put on a couple of pounds due to increased bingeing, and her resolve to try harder to lose weight was not working. In any case, no matter how low her weight was, she always strived to be lighter.

While Emma was keen to expand her pie chart by incorporating other, more helpful aspects by which to judge herself, she was reluctant to give up on controlling her shape and weight, as this was not compatible with her desire to be a model. The therapist doubted that Emma would be able to recover fully from her eating disorder while holding on to this aspiration and made a private note to return to this later in the treatment, as raising this now could have alienated Emma and discouraged her from even trying to alter her self-evaluation system. Instead, the therapist asked Emma to come up with an alternative, more ideal pie chart, with the aim of encouraging her to start making small changes to help her see the benefits of changing her self-evaluation system. Her revised pie chart is shown in Figure 9.8.

While Emma still attached a lot of significance to shape and weight in her revised pie chart, this had reduced considerably and had been replaced by other aspects of her life. Emma acknowledged that she needed to do a lot of work in tackling her overevaluation of shape and weight, and it was agreed that this would be an important focus over the next few weeks. The session then went on to identify ways in which Emma could expand the other, more healthy aspects of her pie chart, such as spending time with friends, even when she did not necessarily feel like it, with the aim of squeezing down the relative importance of shape and weight indirectly.

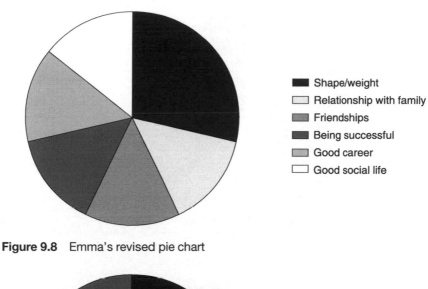

Figure 9.8   Emma's revised pie chart

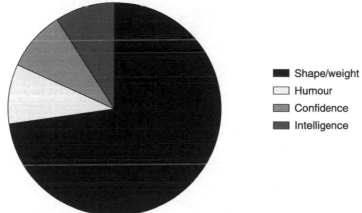

Figure 9.9   Attractiveness pie chart

Using other sorts of pie chart

Once patients understand the concept of pie charts, they can be used cre-atively to examine other concepts, either on their own or alongside other techniques. Consider the belief, 'being thin means being attractive'. In add-ition to using orthogonal lines (described above), 'attractiveness' pie charts can be used to help gather evidence to challenge this belief.

Figure 9.9 demonstrates the initial assumption that shape and weight are the most important attributes in determining a person's attractiveness. Exploration and discussion allows differentiation and expansion of the con-cept of attractiveness (Figure 9.10). Finally, having identified appearance as one factor, it is possible to identify *what* aspects of appearance determine attractiveness (Figure 9.11). This can then be checked out with significant others. It is helpful to ask patients to think about their friends or peer group

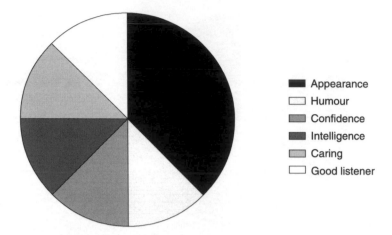

Figure 9.10   Attractiveness pie chart – revised

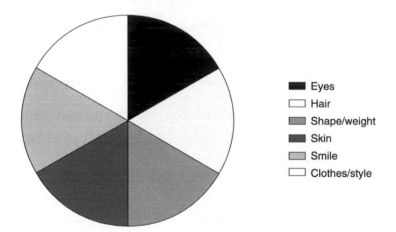

Figure 9.11   Association between appearance and attractiveness

and list what qualities make them attractive – in addition to their enjoying this, using real people helps them to understand the true meaning of attractiveness.

Sometimes, patients do not identify shape and weight as being the most important aspect of their self-evaluation, and this is reflected in their pie chart. This is not necessarily because they are deliberately trying to mislead us, but usually it is because they are judging themselves in other key areas that are linked to the need to control their eating/weight/shape. Conversely, some patients can readily identify eating/weight/shape as being important to them but struggle to identify other important factors that may be contributing to the need for control in this area.

> *Jake, a 14-year-old boy with AN, was well aware of the importance he attached to his appearance (his physique was more important than his*

weight per se, although weight was an indication of whether his shape had changed at any given time). However, he found it difficult to identify other factors that were important in how he judged himself. His therapist used Socratic questioning to elicit when Jake last felt sad and when he last felt happy, and encouraged him to think through why he might have felt that way. Jake recalled that he had been happy a couple of days before when he got a good mark on a school test and his parents and teachers were really pleased with him which made him feel good. He also remembered a difficult football match at the weekend when he had missed a penalty. This had ruined his weekend because his team lost and he felt that he had let everybody down, particularly his dad who had come to watch the match. The therapist asked Jake what he was most upset about: the fact that he could have taken a better kick or the fact that he let others down. Jake said that he felt most bothered that his dad and coach had been disappointed in him. This led to a discussion about Jake's need to please others in order to feel good about himself, which he could relate to and was able to give lots of additional examples.

Although Jake's pie chart looked fairly well balanced, it revealed lots of factors related to pleasing other people; this characteristic was incorporated into his CBT formulation and became the focus of sub-sequent sessions.

Body checking and avoidance

Body checking is a common phenomenon in those with eating disorders and occurs in a variety of ways; most common are scrutinising oneself in mirrors, pinching body parts, repeated weighing, trying on clothes, and making unhelpful comparisons to others. During adolescence in particular, these sorts of behaviours are quite common and to some extent normal; however, for those with eating disorders, the thoughts that drive the behaviours tend to be unhelpful, resulting in a biased interpretation and a negative mood state. Usually, patients are unaware either that they are engaging in the behaviour(s) at all or of the extent to which they are doing so, and they are almost always unaware of the negative consequences associated with the behaviour.

When patients are asked about body checking, they are generally able to identify one or two examples, even though they may downplay the significance of them. In order to get an accurate picture of the extent of body checking, patients should be set a homework task of recording the behaviour in their diary, giving details about what they did and how long they did it for. It is not necessary for patients to record this every day, but it is important that they choose a fairly typical day to record body checking. The therapist should dedicate a large proportion of the following session to exploration of the purpose and effects of body checking, using the diary record as a starting point. Initially, it is important to get young persons' view of why they think they body check. Usually, it is in order to make themselves feel better by reassuring themselves that they are not fat or have not gained weight. The therapist should educate the young person by illustrating, firstly, that, when we are looking for evidence for something, what we find is greatly influenced by our prior beliefs and expectations. This can work in a positive way. For example, if we want to confirm our belief that our favourite band can sound as well live as they do recorded and we strongly expect that to be the case, we are likely to look for evidence of this at the live concert and play down any mistakes. Body checking, however, tends to confirm negative beliefs. For example, if a girl has a strong belief that she is fat and expects to find evidence of this when looking in the mirror, then there is a strong likelihood that she will magnify any signs of this and minimise any counter-evidence.

Patients should also be reminded here that we all have fat/loose skin on our body, and the harder we look for it, the easier it is to find.

As highlighted earlier, it is much harder to disconfirm beliefs than to confirm them, so if we strongly believe something to be true, the chances are we will readily assimilate any information that fits this belief. Ultimately, patients should be encouraged to understand how subjective this experience is and that in order to get an accurate account, a more balanced and object-ive viewpoint is necessary, taking into account all the evidence available. This is much easier to do when we do not care too much about the con-sequences. For example, if we do not care too much about the live band, we may go to the concert and listen for both the good bits *and* the bad bits and discuss this with friends before making a balanced decision as to whether the concert was any good. By the very nature of the eating disorder, patients care about whether or not they are fat or have gained weight. Recovery would be easier if this were not the case; however, it is unrealistic and indeed unhelpful to wait for this to change before tackling body checking behaviours that maintain preoccupation with fatness and weight.

Once patients have identified and recorded the presence of body check-ing, they should be asked to record the effects of it, based on their views about its purpose. For example, if the patient believes that scrutinising her-self in the mirror will reassure her that she is not fat and therefore make her feel better, she should be asked to record this information in the diary after each episode of body checking. For some patients, this task is not necessary, as merely having recorded body checking and discussing the consequences with the therapist may have made them aware that, at best, it has no effect and, at worst, it makes them feel less happy about their body (as well as more generally) and keeps their preoccupation going. In order to obtain a more objective and accurate account, patients should be encouraged to consider all the evidence available to them, in the ways that have been described earlier. While this is best done with the therapist initially, it is helpful for patients to have a copy of the evidence to hand so that they can add to it and remind themselves of it at vulnerable times.

Some patients with eating disorders engage in body avoidance behaviours; for example, wearing lots of layers, not looking in mirrors and avoiding knowing their weight. As with body checking, this is driven by negative beliefs about their body. However, rather than confirming their worst fears by exposing themselves (and others) to their body, they try to make themselves feel better by avoidance. Again, like body checking, this tends not to work because it prevents disconfirmation of beliefs and is similar to the use of safety behaviours in the anxiety field (see Wells, 1997).

> Body checking is dysfunctional by confirming negative beliefs about body shape and appearance

Feeling fat

The sensation of 'feeling fat' is common in females in general, not just those with eating disorders, and it is associated with distress, negative emotions, internal and external body sensations, negative images, negative self-beliefs, and a first memory of feeling fat – these tend to be most pronounced in patients with AN (Cooper *et al.*, 2007). When working with these patients (and in our experience most youngsters with eating disorders experience feeling fat at some point or other), the therapist should try to identify any unhelpful cognitive styles that may be exacerbating the problem, as this will help to direct the choice of intervention. For example, does the patient believe that she is fat (e.g. emotional reasoning – I feel fat therefore I am), or does she continue to strive for thinness despite knowing she is unhealthily thin compared to others (e.g. double standards)? As mentioned earlier, some young people with eating disorders know that they are thin but, paradoxically, feel fat, whereas others not only feel fat but also believe it to be true – either way, there is usually an associated belief that 'I will feel better if I lose more weight', resulting in restricting and other problematic behaviour, and it is this which needs addressing.

In addition to distinguishing between feeling fat and the (faulty) belief of being fat, it is also important to distinguish between being fat and being overweight from a health perspective. While it is helpful to work with unhelpful belief systems in obese patients with eating disorders, additional specialist dietetic and medical help is usually required, and these cases are not considered within this book.

Claire was making reasonably good progress in tackling her eating disorder. However, as she regained the weight she had lost, she complained more and more of feeling fat, despite still having a low BMI and meeting criteria for a diagnosis of AN. The therapist addressed this in the following eight steps:

1   *Monitor. Firstly, it is important for both the patient and therapist to have an understanding of the circumstances surrounding feeling fat, as, while young persons may say that they feel fat all the time, this is almost always more pronounced at certain times of the day or in response to certain situations. Ask the patient to spend a couple of*

days recording when it happens in the diary and then review this in the following session.

2   *Explore what thoughts are triggered by the feeling (e.g. I must lose weight/if I lose weight, I will feel better).*

3   *Encourage the patient to spot any associated unhelpful thinking styles (e.g. I feel fat; therefore I am fat: emotional reasoning).*

4   *Educate: what effect does the feeling have on behaviour? (e.g. restrict intake).*

5   *Explore the impact of responding to the feeling in this way (e.g. does it make you feel better?).*

6   *Incorporate into formulation.*

7   *Challenge/explore the feeling in more detail: could it be a reflection of another feeling? (e.g. anxiety, boredom).*

8   *Can I deal with the 'real' feeling in a more productive way (e.g. problem solving)?*

Identify cognitions associated with the sensation of feeling fat

---

Developing a time line

Once patients have identified and worked on challenging maintaining factors, it is helpful if they have a reasonable understanding of how their over-evaluation of shape and weight developed in the first place. There should already be at least some awareness of this because such information is important when understanding and formulating difficulties. However, up until this point, the main focus of treatment has been on current maintaining thoughts and behaviours. We would argue that understanding the specific *cause* of negative beliefs and problematic behaviour is useful in terms of reducing the likelihood of relapse and helping patients to distance themselves from beliefs that may no longer be relevant. This does not mean it is 'the holy grail' and absolutely necessary for patients to overcome their eating disorder. Discussing early feelings about one's developing body can be extremely anxiety provoking, and it is much more likely that the therapist will be able to elicit this information accurately and sensitively after developing a trusting relationship with the young person. For this reason, we would recommend that this work be done later in treatment. For those who are happy to talk about the subject, this can be done in the session, as in a semi-structured interview with prompt questions. However, we find that asking patients to draw up a time line and make notes based on the prompt questions for homework is a useful exercise. Asking them to bring in photographs and even other relevant objects such as clothes can be especially useful in expressing to patients that the therapist is interested in their 'story' and will encourage them to share their experiences in more detail. The prompt questions should be based on the following areas:

1   own feelings about shape/weight/appearance (e.g. can you remember when you first became dissatisfied with your shape/weight; when did you first start to link being thin with being happy; have you ever felt positive about your shape/weight?)
2   other peoples' attitudes (or perceptions of them) to patient's shape/weight (peers and family in particular; ask about any teasing/negative comments, etc.)
3   family values attached to shape/weight generally (do other family members value thinness; if so, how is this manifested?)
4   impact of overconcern with appearance (e.g. does worrying about your appearance prevent you from doing anything or help you to do anything?).

Once patients have completed this exercise, the therapist should attempt to create a shared understanding with them of why they may have become sensitive to the importance of shape and weight, with the aim of conveying, firstly, that the concerns are understandable and important, but, secondly, that they are unhelpful and need addressing.

> Time lines provide a helpful way of learning how concerns about body shape and appearance developed over time

Working with perfectionism

Perfectionism has long been hypothesised to be a major predisposing factor in the development of eating disorders (e.g. Bruch, 1978; Slade, 1982); indeed, the eating disorder pioneer Hilda Bruch described young AN patients as 'fulfilling every parent's and every teacher's idea of perfection'. Some authors have argued for a distinction between 'normal' perfectionism, defined as striving for reasonable and realistic standards that leads to a sense of self-satisfaction and enhanced self-esteem, and 'neurotic' perfectionism, which is a tendency to strive for excessively high standards and is motivated by fears of failure and worry about letting others down (Flett and Hewitt, 2002). Shafran *et al.* (2002) have given a cognitive-behavioural account of what they call 'clinical' perfectionism, which is intrinsically linked with self-evaluation and the pursuit of personally demanding standards despite adverse consequences. This has recently been proposed as a key maintaining mechanism for severe AN in adults (Fairburn *et al.*, 2003). Specifically, clinical perfectionism is maintained by biased evaluation of performance, reappraising standards as being insufficiently demanding if they are met, reacting to failure with self-criticism, and avoidance of tasks or procrastination in the salient domain(s) (Figure 9.12).

Claire, a 14-year-old girl with AN, came from a high-achieving family and was herself a high-flyer both academically and in sport. Her efforts had been rewarded with lots of positive comments from both teachers and parents and regular school prizes; however, more recently, the head teacher had expressed some concern to her mother that she might be pushing herself too hard and that this seemed to be having a negative impact on her concentration and energy levels in class. She was also finding it increasingly difficult to maintain her high standards because she kept 'moving the goalposts' and setting new challenges for herself. The therapist was aware that Claire had a tendency to complete homework tasks to perfection and that she put a lot of pressure on herself to impress others by doing things well. Claire herself was aware of this desire to do things well, partly for herself and partly because she did not want to let others down, and she saw no problem with this. The therapist

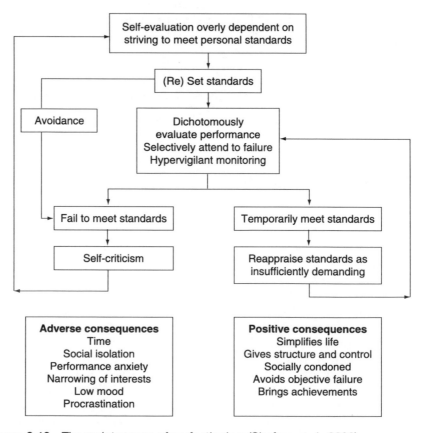

Figure 9.12   The maintenance of perfectionism (Shafran *et al.*, 2002)

reminded Claire of her tendency to bring a 'perfect' diary to the early sessions because she was keen to impress the therapist. Claire recalled that she had got upset when she realised that this was frustrating for her therapist, because it did not give her much to work on; furthermore, it was more stressful to have to devise a perfect diary than it was just to be honest. She had been able to see that not only were her efforts not being rewarded, but they were also counterproductive in several ways. To some extent, Claire's perfectionism enabled her to make some positive changes to her eating because she was keen to recover to the best of her ability and therefore completed homework tasks well. However, it had become apparent that her tendency to be overcritical and focus on what she had not managed to achieve was getting in the way of moving forward with her recovery. The therapist used this information to open up a discussion about Claire's need to be perfect and impress others, and Claire started to consider the possibility that this might be causing problems for her; however, she was not convinced that she was as perfectionistic as her therapist had suggested. Claire's perfectionism and its relation to her eating disorder was formulated as shown in Figure 9.13 (see p. 142).

Perfectionism is manifested by a range of beliefs, conditional assumptions and thinking styles that reinforce the need to strive harder to achieve targets. Such beliefs are addressed in a similar way to other unhelpful beliefs and thinking styles in those with eating disorders. For example, if a patient has the belief, '*I must not eat fattening foods*', the therapist may want to help the patient to generate evidence for and against this belief (using some of the techniques described above) before deciding on whether the belief is valid and useful. Behavioural experiments (for example, incorporating some fattening foods into the diet in moderation and seeing what the impact on weight is) are useful in providing direct feedback and altering the power of the belief. Problematic behaviours serving to maintain the belief (e.g. a tendency to buy lots of diet magazines aimed at helping obese people lose weight) are also addressed.

In Claire's case, the following strategies were adopted to help her to tackle her perfectionism:

1   Detailed discussion of the advantages and disadvantages of perfectionism. *A considerable amount of time was dedicated to exploration of the benefits versus the drawbacks of Claire's perfectionism, in the same way that the pros and cons of the eating disorder per se might be explored early in treatment. The therapist reassured Claire that she did not want her to lose her high standards altogether or change her personality, but rather to take some pressure off her so that she could function to the best of her ability.*

2   Addressing maintaining behaviours. *Claire closely monitored the extent to which she was meeting her goals – for example, checking*

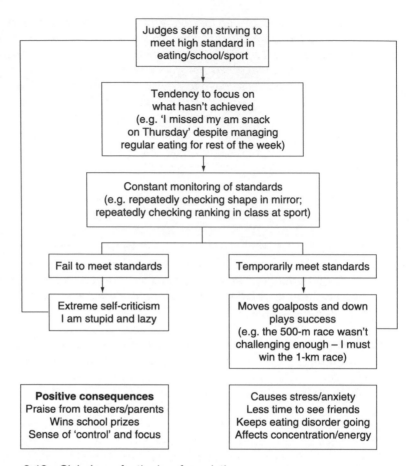

Figure 9.13   Claire's perfectionism formulation

whether she was still top of the class and repeatedly asking her schoolmates how many hours of revision they had done, before making sure she did more. As she had already done some work on body checking (see above), she could understand that this type of checking was probably unhelpful and responded well to the suggestion that she monitor and reduce this in a similar way.

3   Tackling beliefs and unhelpful cognitive styles. *It was acknowledged that a number of unhelpful thinking styles were likely to be maintaining Claire's perfectionism, particularly minimising positives and maximising negatives, and double standards, and these were addressed by some of the techniques described earlier in this chapter.*

4   Historical review of the development of Claire's perfectionism. *Claire's perfectionism was long-standing and seemed – to some degree – to be a family trait, in that both parents seemed to have extremely high standards themselves; indeed, the therapist wondered whether they also had particularly high expectations of their*

daughter. In the same way that a time line might be developed to facilitate understanding about the development of the overevaluation of shape and weight, Claire was asked to make some notes about the development of her need for high standards, based on prompt questions devised by her therapist.

Using the combination of strategies described here, Claire was able, firstly, to acknowledge that she was indeed a perfectionist – an achievement in itself, as, typically, this is denied (how can a 'true' perfectionist ever accept themselves as being one?). Secondly, she was able to see that her perfectionism might be having a detrimental effect, and, thirdly, she was able to tackle this in a way that increased the likelihood of keeping hold of the benefits while reducing the negative consequences. Some might describe this as a shift from 'neurotic' or 'clinical' perfectionism to 'normal' perfectionism.

Perfectionist beliefs need to be acknowledged and challenged

10

Stage 5: relapse prevention and discharge planning

Deciding when to discharge a young person from treatment for an eating disorder can be tricky, due not least to the following three factors:

1   patient uncertainty about whether they will 'cope'
2   parent anxiety about whether they will cope with their child
3   therapist uncertainty about whether sufficient progress has been made.

Timing the discharge

In most cases, worries about potential relapse drive the uncertainty. Some therapists say that discharge planning begins from the start of treatment, whereas others admit to avoiding the topic for fear of raising anxiety in either the patient or the parents – neither approach seems particularly helpful. It is important for patients and their families to be aware that discharge is an inevitable aim of treatment, and the 6-weekly reviews provide an ideal opportunity to put this on the agenda. It makes sense to reduce gradually the frequency of sessions prior to discharge, mainly to encourage the child and her family to see that they can cope without their therapist but also so that any specific difficulties as a result of stopping treatment (such as transferring weighing to the home environment) can be addressed.

What is good enough?

The child should have been completing regular self-report assessment measures throughout treatment, and, together with therapist and parent reports and observations, these should give a reasonably good indication of the level of progress made. In an ideal world, eating disorder patients at discharge would have improved significantly in all domains to the point where no or only a few difficulties are reported. In reality, while this can happen, it rarely does.

The therapist, with the support of the clinical team, needs to decide whether the progress made in treatment is sufficient to warrant discharge, and perhaps the most important question becomes, 'Is this child able to continue making progress *without* active treatment?' Every attempt should be made to encourage the child herself (and, if relevant, parents) to see that any progress made has been primarily a result of *her* hard work, rather than the therapist's, in order to reduce any anxiety about her ability to continue recovering after discharge (thus increasing self-efficacy). In fact, rather than see the recovery process as lasting the duration of the treatment, it is more helpful to see it as a longer-term process, with treatment just comprising the first phase.

It is unlikely that a child attending an outpatient eating disorder clinic would have serious medical complications at this stage of treatment, because these would have warranted earlier medical intervention. However, there may be some residual concerns regarding physical health, such as amenorrhea or problems associated with reduced, but continuing vomiting. In these cases, while discharge from the eating disorder service may still be considered, physical health monitoring would be recommended, and this role is usually taken on by the GP.

In cases where difficulties are more complex, some residual symptoms and problematic behaviours may persist beyond successful treatment of the eating disorder, or new problems may develop as old ones disappear. Rather than attempt to solve all these problems, we generally advise going ahead with the planned discharge, to give young patients a break from treatment and allow them to consolidate what they have learnt. In some cases, referral to another service or therapist may be required to deal with other (co-morbid) difficulties.

> The resolution of all difficulties is rarely achieved before discharge. The decision to discharge is largely determined by the young person's ability to sustain progress

Relapse prevention

Once the child is able to manage her eating disorder to the point where discharge is imminent, the next real challenge begins: maintenance of progress. Some children are confident that having challenged the beliefs and behaviours associated with their eating disorder, they will never go back to their old ways. Sometimes they are right. However, it is important to be realistic about the risk of slipping back into old habits in times of stress, as being prepared for any slip-backs will ensure that they are kept to a minimum should they occur. From the therapist's point of view, it is important to convey a balance between optimism and realism so that the child can feel confident and hopeful of maintaining progress but without the pressure for everything to be perfect from discharge on. Anticipating lapses can also reduce feelings of guilt and hopelessness, should they occur.

Relapse prevention was initially described in relation to substance use (Marlatt and Gordon, 1985) and focuses attention on the identification of high-risk situations likely to trigger problematic behaviour, and on interventions that help patients either to avoid or cope with such situations, hence interrupting the relapse process. This model has been adapted for use in many clinical situations, including eating disorders.

Identifying strategies for maintenance of progress

The first step in completing a relapse-prevention plan should involve a review of what has been helpful in treatment and, specifically, which strategies the young person should continue to use to reduce the likelihood of relapse. This should be a joint exercise between the therapist and young person. However, it is important to remember that, while the therapist may believe that certain aspects of the treatment were helpful, the child may have a different view, and in such cases, unless the therapist is convinced that a particular strategy is crucial to the maintenance of progress (and the task then becomes to persuade the young person of this), these aspects should not be included in the plan.

> Relapse-prevention planning involves the identification of helpful strategies

Jake was originally referred with atypical AN and did well in treatment. Of particular note was Jake's sensitivity to criticism, and this was exacerbated by his father's own sporting and academic success and his high expectations of Jake. At the height of his illness, Jake became very isolated from his friends and had a virtually non-existent social life, apart from attending football training, which he excelled at. He was a worrier, and anxieties about whether he was healthy enough, clever enough, fit enough, attractive enough and so on dominated his thoughts.

Jake's initial relapse prevention plan was as follows:

- *Keep busy.*
- *Stay in touch with friends.*
- *Be sociable.*
- *Concentrate on work but don't put too much pressure on myself to be 'the best'.*
- *Try to achieve for myself first and foremost rather than for others.*
- *Work on expanding 'healthy' aspects of the pie chart.*

- *Address negative feelings as and when they arise.*
- *Keep eating structured (three meals and three snacks).*
- *Continue to eat previously avoided foods in a flexible way.*
- *Resist temptation to weigh myself often (but OK monthly).*
- *Take regular but not driven exercise.*
- *Be aware of and resist temptation to scrutinise body.*
- *Avoid comparing myself to others.*
- *Be flexible and welcome change.*
- *Remember to look for the positive angle when feeling negative.*
- *Find ways to appreciate the here and now.*
- *Don't spend time worrying about the what ifs? at the expense of living my life.*

Identifying high-risk situations

Broadly speaking, it is possible to identify risk situations in three categories:

1 negative emotional states (anxiety, depression, anger, boredom, etc.)
2 conflicts in interpersonal relationships (break-up with boyfriend, row with parents, etc.)
3 external pressures (school exams, forthcoming school prom, etc.).

There is, of course, often some overlap between categories (for example, in the case of a relationship break-up causing boredom and low mood, or anger causing conflict with parents); however, it is useful to have these categories in mind when identifying a list of high-risk situations.

In order to identify personally significant high-risk situations, it is important that the young person have some insight into the development and maintenance of the eating disorder. This work should have already been done within the cognitive behavioural treatment programme and should be consolidated in this last phase of treatment.

While some individuals find it easy to list potentially risky situations, others seem to struggle, and this is a cause for concern in that it may signify a reluctance to accept that there may be times at which they are vulnerable to slipping back. In such cases, it may be helpful to go over old diary entries and formulations as a reminder of potential triggers to problematic eating behaviour. Rather than being an unhelpful reminder of the past, this usually helps young people to see how much progress they have made, and can serve to increase self-efficacy, which is a crucial component of relapse prevention.

When thinking prospectively about risky situations, it is useful to identify a specific time period, say, the next 6–12 months, rather than having a vague idea about potential risks in 5 years' time. While it may be relatively easy for young people to identity external triggers, such as end-of-year exams, which are inevitable and tangible, it can be more difficult for them to identify emotional states. However, hopefully, they will have worked on this area earlier in treatment. Again, the diary can be useful here because it contains the young person's own descriptions of thoughts and feelings that trigger problems.

It is tempting for therapists to list potentially risky situations themselves; however, this is not helpful, as it discourages the child from taking an active approach to reducing the likelihood of relapse. If the young person is struggling, it can be useful to start the process in the session and ask her to continue working on it for homework. If there are still difficulties, some gentle nudging from the therapist may be required; however, in reality, most children are able to come up with a reasonable and realistic list.

> Identify potential risky situations over the coming 6–12 months

Jake's list of high-risk situations was as follows:

- *exam time*
- *the days leading up to an important football match*
- *negative comments from peers (particularly relating to appearance)*
- *negative comments from Dad (particularly relating to his football or grades)*
- *becoming physically ill (leading to overanxiety about his health)*
- *going on holiday (and other changes to daily routine).*

Understanding the warning signs

Once the list is complete, the next step is to understand the warning signs – that is, indications that signify eating behaviour may be becoming problematic. To do this, it may be helpful to go through the risky situations and ask the child, 'What would you have done 6 months ago in response to that situation?' For example, if 'being at a party with lots of attractive thin girls' has been identified as a risky situation, the young person may recall that in a previous situation, this triggered cutting out breakfast and supper, and this could then lead to 'missing out meals/snacks' being identified as a warning sign.

As before, if there are difficulties with this, use the diary as a reminder. While not knowing the answers could mean that patients have moved on so far from the eating disorder that it is nothing but a distant memory, it is more likely that they are avoiding thinking about it, a development that does not bode well for effective relapse prevention. In most cases, children can readily identify old coping behaviours and dismiss them as unhelpful in recovering from their eating disorder.

Another helpful activity is to go through the 'time line' completed earlier in treatment by the child, which gives an overview of how she was before and during her eating disorder. This will enable the child to identify the changes that were happening to her as the eating disorder developed in terms of, for example, behaviours, thoughts and feelings.

Identify warning signals

Fiona, a 17-year-old girl recently recovered from BN, found it difficult to identify warning signs other than 'putting on weight', which was her big fear following discharge. Earlier in treatment, Fiona had completed a time line, which dated back to her early childhood and included photographs as well as written accounts of her life to date. Using this as an aid, Fiona was able to see that prior to the onset of her BN, she looked very thin and was rarely smiling in any of the photographs. While she had learnt during treatment that extreme dieting can cause food cravings and bingeing behaviour, her concern with weight gain had resulted in her overlooking the evidence that weight loss was in fact one of the greatest indicators that she might be losing control over her eating. This reminded Fiona of her preoccupation with diet books and health magazines around that time, as well as her rigid exercise programmes, which she was never able to keep up. She was also aware that while she had made good progress over the last few months, she still had a tendency to eat (and sometimes drink) too much during school holidays or when she was feeling stressed. Her final list of warning signs looked like this:

Fiona's warning signs

- *four consecutive weeks of weight loss*
- *becoming obsessed with exercise*
- *buying lots of diet/health books*
- *becoming isolated from friends/avoiding social occasions*
- *snapping at family/feeling irritated a lot of the time*
- *feeling more miserable than usual*
- *boredom/no structure to day*
- *increased alcohol intake*
- *feeling increasingly stressed.*

Having a clear management plan

The next stage in relapse prevention is helping young persons identify appropriate strategies either to avoid the risky situations or cope with them. It is recommended that these strategies be implemented as 'a way of life', at least for the few months following discharge, in order to give the young person the best chance of maintaining any progress made. Identifying what has been helpful in the recovery process so far is a useful starting point. It is important to listen carefully to the young person and encourage her to elaborate on what has been helpful and why, rather than for the therapist to assume wrongly that certain aspects of treatment have been helpful.

Identify a management plan

Claire, a 14-year-old girl recently recovered from AN, was reasonably confident about maintaining the progress she had made during treatment; however, her mother was anxious about the risk of relapse, particularly as she felt that the eating disorder 'crept up on them' without their noticing. It was agreed that Claire would work out a relapse-prevention plan together with her therapist, and then this would be discussed with her mother, so that she, too, could feel more prepared for the coming months and less anxious about Claire slipping back. When thinking about what had been most helpful during treatment, Claire identified the regular eating plan as crucial. The therapist reminded Claire of how introducing her 'dangerous' foods in a planned, controlled way helped her to increase the variety in her diet that encouraged more flexible eating, and she asked Claire whether she wanted to identify this as something to continue with. Claire felt that while this had been helpful earlier in treatment, it might feel a little too controlled to continue with it at this stage and might even increase her preoccupation with food. Instead, she opted to identify a general guideline to allow herself to eat all foods in moderation. The discussion about being too controlled led to Claire and her therapist exploring the work they had done on perfectionism. Claire had been able to realise that while her high standards and drive to achieve had worked in her favour, her rigid goals in pursuit of achievement in the main had gradually started to have a negative impact on her life. She had made some positive steps in addressing this during treatment, such as learning to appreciate her successes rather than focusing on what she had not achieved and challenging her beliefs about 'success' and 'failure'. Claire had learned a lot about her unhelpful thinking styles during treatment, particularly her tendency to 'filter' and distort information so that negatives were emphasised and attributed to herself, whereas positives were discounted or attributed to external or chance circumstances.

Claire's final list looked like this:

Claire's strategies for maintenance of progress
- *Continue with regular eating (three meals and three snacks).*
- *Allow myself to eat all foods in moderation – nothing is 'forbidden'.*
- *Keep eating 'social' – avoid eating alone.*
- *Resist the temptation to weigh myself more than fortnightly.*
- *Avoid comparing my eating to what others are eating (the information is 'distorted' because I don't have all the facts).*
- *Don't buy 'skinny' jeans in the hope that I will eventually fit into them.*

- *Don't spend more than half an hour getting ready in the morning and avoid scrutinising myself in the mirror.*
- *Don't set rigid rules for schoolwork (e.g. must do 4 hours of revision every night).*
- *Stop second-guessing what others are thinking about me.*
- *Praise myself when I have done something well.*
- *Stop focusing on and blaming myself for the negatives and instead try and be objective about what went wrong.*
- *Remember that being the best is not the most important thing in the world, but being happy is really important.*
- *Do things that I enjoy but that are non-competitive (e.g. salsa classes with friends, play piano for fun).*
- *Talk to mum if I am feeling down – don't bottle feelings up.*

Handling lapses

While not inevitable, lapses following recovery from an eating disorder are not uncommon. As mentioned earlier, preparing the child and her family for lapses is crucial because it is generally not the lapse itself that causes major difficulties but rather the way that it is handled, cognitively, behaviourally and emotionally. For example, consider the scenario of a patient who binged and vomited 3 months after discharge, having not done this for several weeks. Those who have catastrophic and self-blaming thoughts about this ('Treatment has all been for nothing'; 'I'm useless'; 'I will never recover') are likely to feel depressed and hopeless and less motivated to make the appropriate changes, thus increasing the likelihood of this being a self-fulfilling prophecy. However, patients who adopt a more objective and neutral stance ('It's the first binge in ages'; 'It's not the end of the world') are more likely to feel positive about the prospect of getting back on track ('I have done it before – I can do it again') and thus more likely to explore ways in which they can change their behaviour in a positive way.

The relapse plan can and should evolve over time as new information comes to light and new coping strategies are identified following lapses.

> Identify cognitive strategies that will help manage lapses

A couple of months after discharge, Fiona went to a party at a friend's house, which involved a buffet supper and lots of alcohol. Fiona lost control over her eating that evening, and this carried on into the following day. Fiona tried to forget about what had happened; however, she continued to feel bad and this resulted in further bingeing. At the end of the week, Fiona looked at her relapse prevention plan and specifically at the 'handling lapses' section, which looked like this:

- *Identify the trigger(s) to the lapse – be specific.*

- *Do I need to add anything to the 'high-risk situation' or 'strategies for maintaining progress' lists?*
- *Is the problem still there – can I address it by problem solving?*
- *Could I have handled the situation differently – if so, how?*
- *Am I using the strategies identified for maintenance of progress?*
- *Don't catastrophise – it's a minor lapse – I'm still much further on than this time last year.*
- *Start using the diary for a couple of weeks to get back on track with planning and structured eating.*

Fiona noted that she had not been to a buffet for quite some time and assumed that she would be OK. However, she now realised that she should have had 'buffet' on her high-risk situation list, because this situation triggered her anxiety and encouraged her to drink more alcohol, reduced her inhibitions, and ultimately led to her losing control over her eating. Fiona went over her notes about how to handle buffet situations and devised a detailed plan of how to cope with these in the future.

She also realised that she should have spotted the 'lapse' as soon as the binge had occurred that evening, rather than allowing it to continue into the following week, and made a note on her plan to be alert to any lapse and address it quickly, rather than put her head in the sand in the hope that it would go away. Because Fiona did not catastrophise about the situation, she was able to get herself back on track, with the help of her diary and by recapping the strategies she identified as being necessary to maintain her progress.

Follow-up arrangements

The importance of a good follow-up arrangement cannot be overstated, as, in addition to ensuring a commitment from the therapist to the progress of the patient, it reduces any anxieties surrounding discharge. It is important that the initial follow-up appointment is not too close to discharge, to allow sufficient time to consolidate what has been learnt in treatment, but not too far away, as too long a gap may heighten anxieties about being able to cope – a 3-month gap is probably optimal. It should be presented as a helpful opportunity to review progress and address any difficulties that may have arisen rather than a meeting to check that things have not gone down-hill. Sometimes, young people are keen to come back and tell their therapist how things have been, whereas others may be quite reluctant to do this, and understanding the motivation behind this attitude is important to enable the therapist to judge whether to recommend further input or monitoring. Usually, follow-up appointments will be made with the therapist or another member of the eating disorder team; however, it may be that it is more practical for them to happen in another service, such as at the GP surgery, particularly if there are good links with these services and they are aware of the relapse-prevention plan. Sometimes, formal follow-up is not arranged, because either it is not wanted or not required. In any case, it is important that young persons and their parents be aware of the options available to them should they require further input in the future.

> A 3-month follow-up appointment is suggested

Part IV

Applications and challenges

11

Inpatient management, groups and self-help

The approaches we have described in the preceding chapters form the basis of a CBT treatment approach that will meet the needs of many young people with a range of eating disorders. Some, however, will benefit from additional therapeutic help, while others, for a variety of reasons, will be unable or unwilling to commit themselves to the demands of weekly face-to-face appointments.

Additional therapeutic help may take many forms. Some (essentially those with severe AN) may require a spell of inpatient management. Others may benefit from the addition of medication (essentially for co-morbid conditions). Selective serotonin reuptake inhibitor (SSRI) antidepressants, particularly fluoxetine, do, however, appear to have an anti-bulimic action and may be used as an adjunct to CBT.

A certain number of young people ask to be put in touch with others in the same situation as themselves and enjoy sharing experiences and the social benefits of working in a group setting with others. At the other end of the spectrum, some (possibly those living away from home at college, or those who wish to keep their eating disorder more private) wish to tackle their difficulties alone – often in the privacy of their own homes. For these, there are a growing number of self-help resources, delivered by book, CD-ROM or the Internet.

It is beyond the scope of this book to describe the range of treatment approaches in detail, but we will briefly review the application of CBT approaches to the above modes of delivery.

Inpatient management

In theory, inpatient admission might have a role in addressing the physical aspects of eating disorders, as when levels of risk make it hazardous to manage them at home, or to provide intensive psychiatric management. On occasion, admission is proposed because the home situation has become so stressful that the family is at the end of its tether, or cannot provide the level of supervision required. In the UK and a number of other countries (though less so in North America), inpatient psychiatric treatment (often spanning several months) is sometimes considered for those with severe AN. In consequence, a UK audit of occupancy of adolescent inpatient psychiatric units revealed eating disorders to account for the largest number of inpatient bed days by diagnosis (O'Herlihy *et al.*, 2003). A review of the range of alternative service models available and the evidence for them is provided in Gowers and Green (2007).

The NICE guideline has suggested that inpatient management is not recommended for those with bulimia, other than for short-term correction of physical complications.

When a young person is admitted to a medical (paediatric) service for acute physical reasons, psychological therapies might not be the priority, and these can be recommended on discharge, ideally with the therapist keeping in touch during the admission to provide some continuity. If the admission is longer than a week or two, it is reasonable for the CBT programme to be delivered alongside physical management, though young persons are likely to have less input themselves into the feeding and weight restoration aspects of their treatment. In these circumstances, patients' motivation may be affected by their agreement or otherwise with the admission, and this needs to be taken into account in the therapy. If young persons are very opposed to admission, this opposition may damage any motivation, necessitating the therapist to separate the need to address physical aspects of their condition from the therapeutic process aimed at the underlying eating disorder. On the other hand, some young people may passively accept admission, reinforcing any feelings of ineffectiveness or lack of self-esteem, and requiring the therapist to work even harder at addressing these. This raises the question of whether inpatient treatment helps with or, indeed, accelerates progress with CBT or whether it clashes with it. On the whole, our view would be that though sometimes unavoidable and maybe on occasion a life-saving move, admission is, on the whole, a setback to the longer-term aims of recovery, involving additional cognitive and behavioural challenges, rather than a step towards achieving them.

Longer-term psychiatric admission raises similar issues at the outset and additional ones later. It often appears to be more difficult to discharge patients at the end of lengthy treatment than to gain the agreement of a reluctant young person to admission at the outset. Sometimes this seems to be because patients have gained some insights not present at the outset, or that they appreciate therapeutic relationships fostered during the admission. At other times, the reluctance to leave the unit appears to be more based on difficulties of readjustment to the home situation, facing peers after an absence, or a more general lack of confidence. Given that the approach taken in this book is an *active one* in which patients are responsible for and in charge of their treatment, the key to adopting a CBT approach to inpatient management would appear to be to maintain this attitude as far as possible. If inpatient treatment of medical complications is separated from psychiatric admission for treatment of the underlying disorder, it becomes possible to apply some guidelines on psychiatric admission to ensure that the therapeutic aims of admission conform to the overall treatment principles.

These guidelines might include as many of the following as is feasible:

- Treatment is with the young person's agreement.
- The focus of treatment is the young person's thoughts and behaviour, with medical issues being peripheral (though very important), rather than central.
- Weight gain is crucial, but as an *indicator*, rather than the end in itself.
- As behavioural change is important, the young person must play a part in this change – at some stage. This may not be possible at the outset, but must be introduced as early as possible.
- Although food might be provided without negotiation, young persons make an *agreement* at the outset that they will eat (or at least try to eat) what is provided.
- Eating (or not) is a *decision* young persons make (albeit a difficult one). Therefore, the aim of treatment is not to help them eat, but to support the decision to eat.
- The inpatient stay is *conditional* and regularly reviewed.
- The stay is extended because it is achieving results rather than because it is not (see Geller (2005) for discussion of therapist investment in treatment).
- There is good integration with outpatient CBT therapy, before and after admission.

Many who work with motivational approaches separate negotiable from non-negotiable aspects of treatment. The balance may vary with the severity of the disorder, the motivational stage, and, to some extent, the age of the patient. Adding negotiables is important in maintaining the young person's self-esteem and effectiveness. Strict behavioural programmes involving rewards and withdrawal of privileges are not appropriate (and ineffective), so use of leisure time and possibly supportive use of medication may be negotiable. However, negotiating in some areas does not weaken control over non-negotiables.

> Inpatient management is sometimes of benefit, where physical risk is significant. Distinguishing negotiable from non-negotiable aspects is recommended as part of a motivational approach to treatment

Group CBT approaches

Group CBT applications for adolescents have received a lot of attention in recent years for a range of disorders including depression and anxiety as well as eating disorders. Sometimes these are offered as an alternative to individual approaches, but more commonly in the eating disorders field, they are offered as an adjunct. Stewart *et al.* (2007) have highlighted some of the potential advantages of a group approach.

Advantages

- *Cost*.
- *Opportunity to observe and monitor social functioning*.
- *Psychoeducation*: this can be useful for discussing physical effects of eating disorders and facilitating *skills acquisition*.
- *Social support* (and comparing experience).
- *Opportunity to practise new skills*, such as problem solving.
- *Motivation*: young people may motivate each other better than a therapist might, particularly when more experienced group participants demonstrate their progress to new group members.

As with any group therapy, the group can be open or closed. In the former (and this tends to be particularly applicable to an inpatient setting), new members can join at any time and may benefit from the progress and gains of more experienced members. Closed groups tend to have a set number of sessions, offer a greater opportunity to develop a group identity and unity, and enable the therapists to deliver a therapeutic programme sequentially. In a *rotating group*, a series of maybe 10 topics can be delivered, with members joining at any time and leaving when they have completed the cycle. Bloomgarden *et al.* (2007) advocate using a closed group for young people with eating disorders to ensure the development of emotional safety, though this is more difficult to implement in an inpatient setting.

Agenda setting

Whatever the form of the group, a CBT group should follow an agenda as with individual work, with some flexibility permitted to allow processes generated by participants to emerge. The agenda will include introductions and checking in, planning for the session, and setting and reviewing the last session's homework.

Although not widely evaluated, self-help groups focusing on psychoeducation appear to have promising results with older clients (e.g. Olmsted *et al.*, 1991).

> Group CBT can usefully be added as an adjunct to individual therapy

The following are two examples of group exercises that offer a different approach to discussions about food, diets and dieting from what can be addressed in individual sessions.

Exercise: to review the media portrayal of diets and food types with reference to popular magazines.

Group members are invited to bring in a selection of magazines for this exercise.

- What sorts of promises do the articles make about dieting and what style of advertising do they use to promote them?
- How are celebrities who have lost or gained weight portrayed in the magazines.
- Are there any articles on ways to increase weight (where desirable) and the adverse effects of not eating enough for your needs?
- How do these articles affect the way you view food?
- How do these messages compare to the messages you hear in therapy?

It is often apparent that celebrities are criticised for weight loss, while attitudes to plumper female shapes are mixed.

The second exercise aims to address the young people's knowledge about the effects of starvation, both physically and psychologically (in terms of preoccupation with eating, poor concentration and other thought processes).

Exercise: to explore the effects of starvation on physical, psychological and social development with reference to two characters 'Sam' and 'Samantha' (Figure 11.1).

- The outlines of two characters (one thin – Sam – and one healthy – Samantha) are sketched on large sheets of paper.
- The facial features, internal organs (liver, kidneys, heart, etc.) and a sample muscle are drawn separately and pasted onto the figures.
- Flag labels and Post-it notes highlight the consequences of starvation on each body system and on social functioning in Sam.
- The physical and psychosocial changes produced in recovery are attached to Samantha.
- The caricatures can be pinned on the wall for future reference.

This exercise is best done as a fairly light-hearted group exercise, making

Figure 11.1   Sam

the figures look amusing, but with important underlying messages. It is important for the therapists not to be too prescriptive about the benefits of weight gain, but permit some ambivalence to emerge in the labelling of the characters.

Figure 11.1 Samantha

> Group CBT exercises can address important issues in a light-hearted
> manner, using a range of creative techniques

Self-help

A number of self-help CBT packages have been developed for those with
eating disorders, though these are generally for adults or older adolescents.
They are delivered as 'guided self-help' or 'pure' self help – in book form, on
CD-ROM or more recently via the Internet. These approaches are primarily
for BN and are largely untested in low-weight subjects. Pure self-help
involves participants working through module-based worksheets in a book
on their own, and this clearly requires a good deal of motivation.

In guided self-help, subjects may attend a health service setting to work
through CBT exercises at a set time, or with support from a staff member if
they require it. A number of CBT self-help books – for example, those by
Fairburn (1995) and Schmidt and Treasure (1993) – have been evaluated in
clinical trials with promising results for the subgroup (of largely adult
patients) who choose to work in this way, or who may take the opportunity
to start addressing difficulties while on a waiting list for more conventional
therapy. Both have an accompanying volume for clinicians.

Interactive CD-ROM CBT programmes have yielded promising results.
Overcoming Bulimia, for example, comprises eight interactive, multimedia,
CBT sessions, combining cognitive-behavioural, motivational, and educational strategies. It was piloted in two cohort studies in adults with BN,
with good outcomes (Bara-Carril *et al.*, 2004; Murray *et al.*, 2007), and a
recent randomised, controlled trial in adults with BN (Schmidt *et al.*, 2007).

Internet-based programmes (such as the version of *Overcoming Bulimia*
piloted in the Bulimia in Young People Treated Early (BYTE) programme),
may be supported by a peer messaging forum and by therapist email
support. In the BYTE programme (Pretorius *et al.*, submitted), 102 adolescents with BN were recruited either through secondary care services or
through bEAT, the UK eating disorder charity. The uptake of the programme was variable as was the use of the clinician and peer support.
However, when the programme was followed, the clinical gains were good,
suggesting that for a subgroup who do not wish to attend clinical services
and who have access to private Internet facilities, the flexibility this approach
offers may be effective.

> Self-help CBT, delivered by manual or through the Internet, offers an
> alternative for well-motivated young people

12

Future challenges

At present, CBT has a very limited evidence base on which to make recommendations for the treatment of young people with eating disorders. Family-based therapy has a greater, though not exceptionally strong literature to support it and is often regarded as the treatment of choice, despite its lack of a strong theoretical basis. More importantly, it does not offer a practical means of addressing the core cognitions that underlie the condition.

There are the following three main (overlapping) challenges to the establishment of CBT as a significant (or indeed the leading) contributor to this field:

1 clinical challenges
2 research issues
3 challenges in service delivery.

Clinical challenges

CBT has a strong position as the treatment of choice for adults with bulimic disorders. The main clinical challenges we are faced with are to adapt established CBT programmes to the type of eating disorders seen in young people and to make them age-appropriate.

Early-onset eating disorders

Bulimic disorders (especially full-syndrome BN and binge-eating disorder) are rare presentations to child and adolescent mental health services. Much more common are 'atypical eating disorders' and to some extent AN. Many of the atypical disorders occur at low weight. The adult literature has recently introduced the concept of 'transdiagnostic' therapy (Fairburn *et al.*, 2003), and while this is in the early stages of evaluation, it is encouraging to see that CBT programmes for low-weight disorders can apparently incorporate modifications which address the need for weight gain and challenge the specific accompanying cognitions.

In the child and adolescent age group, the common associated features of eating disorders are also somewhat different, whether or not these are seen as constituting full co-morbid conditions. Where obsessive-compulsive features occur (and these seem more common in younger boys), appropriate adjustments will have to be made to CBT programmes, while social communication difficulties, which seem to also be a prominent feature of younger cases, might require attention in order that these can be accommodated within the treatment session. These difficulties will also require attention when planning homework tasks.

Developmental modifications

The issue of age appropriateness has a number of facets. It has a bearing on the style of therapy employed, the language used and the CBT materials to support it. These are all, as we have discussed, likely to be different from those required for adult therapy.

The relationship between therapist and patient is also different in a number of respects, and, crucially, this includes the power relationship. The relationship between an adult therapist and a child cannot be as equal as it is in the adult context, and a key to successful therapy includes using but not abusing adult authority. In modifying adult programmes for adolescents, it is important therefore to take into account the young person's age and consider the ethical basis behind expectations of behaviour modification and requests to complete homework tasks.

The need for age-appropriate modification also relates to the developmental issues underlying and consequent on the eating disorder. For example, issues such as maturity fears, physical and psychological aspects of developing sexuality, and their social implications are often especially prominent in work with this age group.

There are also issues relating to incomplete physical development, of which growth is of major importance. This impact may take a number of forms. Some young people will be concerned about stunting of growth, while others may see this as fulfilling a desire to remain dependent and childlike. Those who are very tall may welcome the curb on further growth that AN affords (Joughin *et al.*, 1992). In treatment, any psycho-educational components will need to take into account the young person's age and the various potential, long-term implications of stunting of physical development. In the treatment of AN, incomplete development has implications for changing weight targets, both with age, as norms increase year on year, and as catch-up growth in height is achieved. The 'moving goalposts' of normal weight add an additional motivational challenge, given that some patients may feel they are committing themselves to an unspecified target, or they may feel the therapist is not being completely candid about the aims and likely outcomes of treatment.

We have discussed throughout this book that 'age appropriateness' also has a bearing on issues of responsibility and the involvement (or otherwise) of other family members (particularly parents). It is simplistic to suggest that empowering parents readily leads to effective behavioural control (and weight gain where this is required). Nevertheless, strengthening the role of parents is often a worthy aim. There is a balance, however, between achieving a situation in which the young person's eating and weight is entirely under parental control (but with no psychological adjustment) and one in which the young person has a better insight and is in control, but weight gain is unreliable. Again, the age of the patient will be an important determinant here.

On the positive side, CBT is widely employed in the management of a range of disorders presenting to CAMHS, and the sensitive involvement of parents is second nature to most services. The behavioural aspects of management are generally easier to address than the cognitive. Treatment in child psychiatry, for disorders such as enuresis, school refusal and hyperkinetic disorder, has a very long history of behavioural management, with parents and others contributing. Cognitive therapy requires a greater degree of developmental sophistication. Adults with eating disorders commonly complain that behavioural and physical change has outpaced any change in their thoughts, and children and adolescents are even more likely to be concerned on this account. It is a major challenge to practitioners to develop CBT in ways that address the cognitive issues underlying eating disorders in this age group.

> The establishment of CBT as a leading therapy for child and adolescent eating disorders will require a focus on the specific developmental and clinical features of this age group

Research challenges

Conducting effective research in child and adolescent mental health poses a number of challenges. Children's age and developmental maturity limit their capacity to consent to any treatment. If a research treatment is proposed, this raises extra consent issues, which cannot be resolved merely by obtaining a parent's consent. Recent changes in the law in England and Wales propose limiting parents' ability to consent to treatment on their children's behalf. It may be that this increases the use of compulsory treatment (under the Mental Health Act) where consent is not forthcoming. Clearly, this will not facilitate the delivery of research-based treatments, delivered through treatment trials. When the treatment involves a condition such as an eating disorder, in which subjects are likely to be ambivalent about their wish to relinquish the disorder and to engage in treatment (of whatever form), further obstacles arise. It is often a step too far, having persuaded young persons to accept a treatment, to expect them to accept one allocated at random in a controlled trial. Research ethics committees, understandably, seek reassurances about the processes involved in eliciting a young person's consent.

Recruitment

Eating disorders in full form are not especially common. Conducting treatment research in AN in particular, requires a multi-centre study to achieve adequately powered recruitment. Recruitment to studies has further problems too. It might be only a minority of potential candidates who would agree to take part in a treatment trial, making recruitment slow. But those who do agree may well be self-selected and therefore atypical. Although some variables such as weight, BMI and frequency of compensatory behaviours might be readily measurable and demonstrate levels of morbidity, it might be that it is the more intangible issues, such as motivation, that predict agreement to participate, but also to achieve a good outcome.

Adherence to treatment

Retaining patients in treatment can be difficult at the best of times, but an additional problem in this field arises when physical concerns necessitate withdrawal from assigned treatment or the addition of a major therapeutic modality. In AN, it is the decision to admit to hospital that often makes interpretation of research findings difficult, particularly when this occurs more commonly in one treatment arm than another. For example, an American study compared a family-based treatment similar to the Maudsley method with a psychodynamically oriented treatment, in which adolescent patients were seen individually with occasional supportive sessions for their parents (Robin *et al.*, 1999). The outcome of both groups was good, both at the end of treatment and 1 year later. However, it is not possible to attribute this finding to one or other of the psychological therapies, as many of the patients were hospitalised during their treatment, and this was especially common among those who received the family therapy.

The TOuCAN trial (Byford *et al.*, 2007; Gowers *et al.*, 2007) is an example of a trade-off between high recruitment and lower adherence to treatment. This multi-centre trial achieved a high rate of recruitment ($n = 215$ cases of DSM-IV AN), representing more than 80 per cent of cases known to community child and adolescent mental health services, covering a population of 7 million. The subjects were therefore typical in every respect. Nearly 80 per cent initially accepted randomisation to in- or out-patient treatment, but subsequent adherence was relatively poor, and there was a high level of crossover between treatments by the time of 2-year follow-up.

Purity of intervention

If a trial aims to investigate the effectiveness of CBT, it is clearly important that the therapists are well trained and that there are in-built quality checks that the therapy given is as planned. Treatment in child and adolescent psychiatry is generally multi-disciplinary and multi-modal where complex disorders are concerned; establishing the impact of the specific therapy under consideration is therefore quite problematic. An efficacy trial may have the benefit of purity, but the findings may bear little relationship to practice in the real world.

> Clinical trials face complex but not insurmountable challenges

Service delivery for CBT programmes

There are a number of reasons why young people with eating disorders do not batter down the doors of clinical services demanding evidence-based treatments. Some of the explanation is within the young people themselves, and some in the nature of existing services.

Young people do not readily seek treatment for any medical problem; they often find that arranging appointments and speaking to adults about personal matters seems to add to their difficulties rather than reduce them. We have discussed at length reasons why those with eating disorders might be especially reluctant to come forward. In consequence, adolescents with mental health problems, and those with eating disorders specifically, might be considered a very hard-to-reach patient group.

If we have a potentially effective treatment approach, but cannot get patients through the door, it suggests that we need to look at the service design and delivery issues that might act as obstacles to engaging patients. If specialised treatments are delivered in secondary care, we need to examine the quality of primary care services in identifying young people with eating disorders and referring on where appropriate.

Primary care

Primary care services delivered in the UK are often perceived by adolescents as unsuitable to meet their needs. They are not specifically designed for this age group, the system for booking appointments is often experienced as inconvenient, and young people often fear that their attendance will not be private or confidential, especially if they are required to take time out of education to attend appointments that are only available during office hours.

The NICE guideline (NICE, 2004) endorsed a number of key principles for the provision of eating disorder services in the UK, and the extent to which recommended practice is being delivered has been examined by two recent studies.

To coincide with the first anniversary of the publication of the NICE guideline, 1700 members of the Eating Disorders Association (now bEAT) and other people affected by eating disorders, including sufferers, carers and professionals, completed a health check card (EDAUK, 2005): 42 per cent of respondents considered that early diagnosis and assessment by GPs was unsatisfactory.

A subsequent three-stage survey of all general practitioners in the South Thames Region ($n = 3783$) found that only 4 per cent of GPs reported using a published guideline or protocol for managing eating disorders (Currin *et al.*, 2006).

Given the apparent deficiencies in primary care, are formal health services the best gatekeepers to effective CBT programmes? Following initiatives in the child obesity field, there is great potential to deliver school-based interventions aimed at prevention and early treatment. These could theoretically introduce CBT concepts and act as more accessible pathways to more intensive treatment. In Chapter 11, we discussed some of the applications (specifically the use of self-help manuals and the Internet) that have been devised to deliver CBT programmes. These may offer complete and effective treatment to some, but, for others, they may be more useful as a first step to treatment, breaking down some of the barriers to formal treatment, reducing some of the fears about engaging with treatment, and increasing motivation.

Secondary care

When young people with eating disorders negotiate primary care and are in need of secondary services, these are often in short supply or, indeed, unavailable; 55 per cent of those completing the EDAUK 'health check' believed that the availability of specialist care was unsatisfactory. Effective CBT programmes can only be delivered if staff are trained effectively to deliver them, and staff training has quite extensive resource implications.

> Effective service delivery requires attention to identification in primary care, and a focus on engagement and adherence to effective treatment

References

American Psychiatric Association (APA) (1994). *Diagnostic and statistical manual of mental disorders* (4th edn) (DSM-IV). Washington, DC: American Psychiatric Association.

Angold, A., Costello, E.J., Messer, S.C., Pickles, A., Winder, F. and Silver, D. (1995). The development of a short questionnaire for use in epidemiological studies of depression in children and adolescents. *International Journal of Methods in Psychiatric Research*, 5, 237–249.

Asen, E. (2002). Outcome research in family therapy. *Advances in Psychiatric Treatment*, 8, 230–238.

Bara-Carril, N., Williams, C.J., Pombo-Carril, M.G., Reid, Y., Murray, K., Aubin S., *et al.* (2004). A preliminary investigation into the feasibility and efficacy of a CD-ROM-based cognitive-behavioral self-help intervention for bulimia nervosa. *International Journal of Eating Disorders*, 35, 538–548.

Beck, A. (1976). *Cognitive therapy and the emotional disorders*. New York: New American Library.

Beck, A.T. and Emery, G., with Greenberg, R.L. (1985). *Anxiety disorders and phobias. A cognitive perspective*. New York: Basic Books.

Bloomgarden, A., Mennuti, R., Conti, A. and Weller, A. (2007). A relational-cultural cognitive-behavioural approach to treating female adolescent eating disorders. In R. Christner, J. Stewart and A. Freeman (eds) *Handbook of cognitive behaviour group therapy with children and adolescents* (pp. 447–464). New York: Routledge.

Bruch, H. (1978). *The golden cage: the enigma of anorexia nervosa*. Cambridge, MA: Harvard University Press.

Bryant-Waugh, R. and Kaminsky, Z. (1993). Annotation: eating disorders in childhood and adolescence. *Journal of Child Psychology and Psychiatry*, 36, 191–202.

Bulik, C.M., Sullivan, P.F., Wade, T. and Kendler, K.S. (2000). Twin studies of eating disorders: a review. *International Journal of Eating Disorders*, 27, 1–20.

Byford, S., Barrett, B., Roberts, C., Clark, A., Edwards, V., Smethurst, N. *et al.* (2007). Economic evaluation of a randomised controlled trial for adolescent anorexia nervosa – the TOuCAN trial. *British Journal of Psychiatry*, 19, 436–440.

Cole, T.J., Freemen, J.V. and Preece, M.A. (1995). *Body mass index reference curves for the UK 1990*. London: Child Growth Foundation.

Cooper, M., Deepak, K., Grocutt, E. and Bailey, E. (2007). The experience of 'feeling fat' in women with anorexia nervosa, dieting and non-dieting women: an exploratory study. *European Eating Disorders Review*, *15*, 366–372.

Cooper, Z. and Fairburn, C.G. (1987). The Eating Disorders Examination: a semi-structured interview for the assessment of the specific psychopathology of eating disorder. *International Journal of Eating Disorders*, *6*, 1–8.

Crisp, A.H. (1994). *Anorexia nervosa – let me be* (2nd edn). London: Academic Press.

Crisp, A.H., Norton, K.W.R., Gowers, S.G., Halek, C., Levett, G., Yeldham, D., *et al.* (1991). A controlled study of the effect of therapies aimed at adolescent and family psychopathology in anorexia nervosa. *British Journal of Psychiatry*, *159*, 325–333.

Currin, L., Schmidt, U., Yeomans, M., Ellis, G., Nodder, J., Stone, C., *et al.* (2006). *Entry into specialist services for the eating disorders: audit of clinical pathways through primary and secondary care*. Report from the Specialist Clinical Audit Programme for South London, Kent, Surrey and Sussex. Bexley, UK: NHS Specialist Clinical Audit Office.

Dare, C. and Eisler, I. (2000). A multi-family group day treatment programme for adolescent eating. *European Eating Disorders Review*, *8*, 4–18.

Dare, C., Eisler, I., Russell, G., Treasure, J. and Dodge, L. (2001). Psychological therapies for adults with anorexia nervosa: randomised controlled trial of outpatient treatments. *British Journal of Psychiatry*, *178*, 216–221.

DiClemente, C. and Prochaska, J.O. (1998). Towards a comprehensive, transtheoretical model of change. In W. Miller and N. Heather (eds) *Treating addictive behaviours* (pp. 3–24). New York: Plenum Press.

Drinkwater, J. (2004). Cognitive case formulation. In P. Graham (ed.) *Cognitive behaviour therapy for children and families* (2nd edn). Cambridge: Cambridge University Press.

Ebeling, H., Tapanainen, P., Joutsenoja, A., Koshinen, M., Morin-Papunen, L., Jarvi, L., *et al.* (2003). *Practice guideline for treatment of eating disorders in children and adolescents*. Helsinki: Finish Medical Association.

EDAUK (2005). Health Check Report: Getting better? Is the quality of treatment for eating disorders in the UK getting better? London: EDAUK. *www.edauk.com*.

Eells, T.D. (ed.) (1997). *Handbook of psychotherapy case formulation*. New York: Guilford Press.

Eisler, I. (2005). The empirical and theoretical base of family therapy and multiple family day therapy for adolescent anorexia nervosa. *Journal of Family Therapy*, *27*, 104–131.

Eisler, I., Dare, C., Hodes, M., Russell, G.F.M., Dodge, E. and Le Grange, D. (1997). Family and individual therapy in anorexia nervosa: a 5-year follow-up. *Archives of General Psychiatry*, *54*, 1025–1030.

Eisler, I., Dare, C., Hodes, M., Russell, G.F.M., Dodge, E. and Le Grange, D. (2000). Family therapy for adolescent anorexia nervosa: the results of a controlled comparison of two family interventions. *Journal of Child Psychology and Psychiatry*, *41*, 727–736.

Epstein, N., Bishop, D. and Levin, S. (1983). The McMaster Family Assessment Device. *Journal of Marital and Family Therapy*, *9*, 171–180.

Fairburn, C.G. (1995). *Overcoming binge eating*. New York: Guilford Press.

Fairburn, C.G. (2007). CBT for eating disorders: principles and procedures. Workshop presented in Truro, Cornwall, UK, April. In G. Waller, H. Cordery,

E. Corstorphine, H. Hinrichsen, R. Lawson, V. Mountford, *et al.* (eds) *Cognitive behavioral therapy for eating disorders: a comprehensive treatment guide.* Cambridge: Cambridge University Press.

Fairburn, C. and Beglin, S.J. (1994). The Eating Disorders Examination Questionnaire. *International Journal of Eating Disorders, 16,* 4, 363–370.

Fairburn, C.G., Cooper, Z., Doll, H. and Welch, S. (1999). Risk factors for anorexia nervosa: a community based case-control study. *Archives of General Psychiatry, 56,* 468–476.

Fairburn, C.G., Cooper, Z. and Shafran, R. (2003). Cognitive behaviour therapy for eating disorders: a transdiagnostic theory and treatment. *Behaviour Research and Therapy, 41,* 509–528.

Fairburn, C.G. and Harrison, P.J. (2003). Eating disorders. *Lancet, 361,* 407–416.

Fairburn, C.G., Welch, S.L., Doll, H., Davies, B. and O'Connor, M.E. (1997). Risk factors for bulimia nervosa. *Behaviour Research and Therapy, 37,* 1–13.

Flett, G. and Hewitt, P. (2002). *Perfectionism: theory, research, and treatment.* Washington, DC: American Psychiatric Association.

Garner, D., Olmsted, M.P. and Polivy, J. (1983). Development and validation of a multidimensional eating disorders inventory for anorexia nervosa and bulimia. *International Journal of Eating Disorders, 2,* 15–34.

Garner, D.M. (2004). *Eating Disorder Inventory-3.* Odessa, FL: Psychological Assessment Resources.

Geller, J. (2002). What a motivational approach is and what a motivational approach isn't: reflections and responses. *European Eating Disorders Review, 10,* 3, 155–160.

Geller, J. (2005). Working relationships: what level of investment is optimal for our clients? Paper presented at London International Conference on Eating Disorders, April 2005.

Geller, J, Williams, K. and Srikameswaran, S. (2001). Clinician stance in the treatment of chronic eating disorders. *European Eating Disorders Review, 9,* 6, 365–373.

Gemelli, R. (1996). Adolescent phase of mental development: age 12 years to age 19 years. In R. Gemelli (ed.) *Normal child and adolescent development* (pp. 445–552). Washington, DC: American Psychiatric Press.

Gowers, S.G. and Bryant-Waugh, R. (2004). Management of child and adolescent eating disorders: the current evidence base and future directions. *Journal of Child Psychology and Psychiatry, 45,* 63–83.

Gowers, S.G., Clark, A., Roberts, C., Griffiths, A., Edwards, V., Bryan, C., *et al.* (2007). Two year outcomes of a randomised controlled trial for adolescent anorexia nervosa. *British Journal of Psychiatry, 19,* 427–435.

Gowers, S.G. and Green, L. (2007). Models of service delivery. In A. Jaffa (ed.) *Eating disorders in children and adolescents* (pp. 248–259). Cambridge: Cambridge University Press.

Gowers, S.G., Harrington, R., Whitton, A., Lelliott, P., Wing, J., Beevor, A. *et al.* (1999). A brief scale for measuring the outcomes of emotional and behavioural disorders in children: HoNOSCA. *British Journal of Psychiatry, 174,* 413–416.

Gowers, S.G., Levine, W., Bailey-Rogers, S., Shore, A. and Burhouse, E. (2002). The use of a routine self-report outcome measure (HoNOSCA-Sr) in two adolescent mental health services. *British Journal of Psychiatry, 180,* 266–269.

Gowers, S., Norton, K., Halek, C. and Crisp, A.H. (1994). Outcome of outpatient psychotherapy in a random allocation treatment study of anorexia nervosa. *International Journal of Eating Disorders, 15,* 165–177.

Gowers, S.G. and Shore, A. (2001). Weight and shape concerns in the development of adolescent anorexia nervosa. *British Journal of Psychiatry*, *179*, 236–242.

Gowers, S.G. and Smyth, B. (2004). The impact of a motivational assessment interview on initial response to treatment in adolescent anorexia nervosa. *European Eating Disorders Review*, *12*, 87–93.

Gowers, S.G., Weetman, J., Shore, A., Hossain, F., and Elvins, R. (2000). The impact of hospitalisation on the outcome of adolescent anorexia nervosa. *British Journal of Psychiatry*, *176*, 138–141.

Graham, P. (2005). *Cognitive behaviour therapy with children and families*. Cambridge: Cambridge University Press.

Harrington, R., Whittaker, J., Shoebridge, P., and Campbell, F. (1998). Systematic review of the efficacy of CBT in childhood and adolescent depressive disorder. *British Medical Journal*, *316*, 1559–1563.

Herzog, D.B., Keller, M.B., Sacks, N.R., Yeh, C.J. and Lavori, P.W. (1992). Psychiatric co-morbidity in treatment-seeking anorexics and bulimics. *Journal of the American Academy of Child and Adolescent Psychiatry*, *31*, 810–818.

Herzog, W., Rathner, G. and Vandereycken, W. (1992). Long term course of anorexia nervosa. A review of the literature. In W. Herzog, J. Detre and W. Vandereycken (eds) *The course of eating disorders* (pp. 15–29). Berlin: Springer Verlag.

Joughin, N., Varsou, E., Gowers, S.G. and Crisp, A.H. (1992). Relative tallness in anorexia nervosa. *International Journal of Eating Disorders*, *12*, 2, 195–207.

Le Grange, D., Eisler, I., Dare, C. and Russell, G.F.M. (1992). Evaluation of family therapy in anorexia nervosa: a pilot suede. *International Journal of Eating Disorders*, *12*, 347–357.

Lock, J., Agras, W.S., Bryson, S. and Kraemer, H.C. (2005). A comparison of short and long term family therapy got adolescent anorexia nervosa. *Journal of the American Academy of Child and Adolescent Psychiatry*, *44*, 632–639.

Lock, J., Le Grange, D., Agras, W. and Fairburn, C. (2001). *Treatment manual for anorexia nervosa; a family based approach*. New York: Guilford Press.

Mahoney, M. (1991). *Human change processes*. New York: Basic Books.

Maloney, M.J., McGuire, J.B. and Daniels, S.R. (1988). The Children's Eating Attitudes Test (ChEAT). *Journal of the American Academy of Child and Adolescent Psychiatry*, *5*, 541–543.

March, J.S. (1995). Cognitive-behavioural psychotherapy in children and adolescents with OCD: a review and recommendations for treatment. *Journal of the American Academy of Child and Adolescent Psychiatry*, *34*, 7–18.

Marlatt, G.A. and Gordon, J.R. (1985). *Relapse prevention: maintenance strategies in the treatment of addictive behaviours*. New York: Guilford Press.

Meads, C., Gold, L. and Burls, A. (2001). How effective is outpatient care compared to inpatient care for treatment of anorexia nervosa? A systematic review. *European Eating Disorders Review*, *9*, 229–241.

Miller, W.R. (1983). Motivational interviewing with problem drinkers. *Behavioural Psychotherapy*, *11*, 147–172.

Miller, W.R. (1994). Motivational interviewing. III. On the ethics of motivational intervention. *Behavioural and Cognitive Psychotherapy*, *22*, 111–123.

Morgan, H.G. and Hayward, A.E. (1988). Clinical assessment of anorexia nervosa. The Morgan-Russell Outcome Assessment Schedule. *British Journal of Psychiatry*, *152*, 367–372.

Murray, K., Schmidt, U., Pombo-Carril, M.G., Grover, M., Alenya, J., Treasure, J., *et al.* (2007). Does therapist guidance improve uptake, adherence and outcome from a CD-ROM based cognitive-behavioral intervention for the treatment of bulimia nervosa? *Computers in Human Behavior*, *23*, 850–859.

NCCMH (National Collaborating Centre for Mental Health) (2004). *Eating disorders: core interventions in the treatment and management of anorexia nervosa, bulimia nervosa and related eating disorders; a National Clinical Practice Guideline*. London: National Institute of Clinical Excellence.

NICE (2004). *Treatment of anorexia nervosa, bulimia nervosa and related eating disorders: a clinical guideline*. London: National Institute for Clinical Excellence.

Nicholls, D. and Bryant-Waugh, R. (2003). Children and young adolescents. In J. Treasure, U. Schmidt and E. Van Furth (eds) *Handbook of eating disorders* (2nd edn, pp. 415–434). Chichester: Wiley.

Nielsen, S., Moller-Madsen, S., Isager, T., Jorgensen, J., Pagsberg, K. and Theander, S. (1998). Standardized mortality in eating disorders – a quantitative summary of previously published and new evidence. *Journal of Psychosomatic Research*, *44*, 413–434.

North, C.D., Gowers, S.G. and Byram, V. (1997). Family functioning and life events in the outcome of adolescent anorexia nervosa. *British Journal of Psychiatry*, *171*, 545–549.

O'Connor, T. and Creswell, C. (2004). Cognitive behaviour therapy in developmental perspective. In P.J. Graham (ed.) *Cognitive behaviour therapy for children and families* (2nd edn, pp. 25–47). Cambridge: Cambridge University Press.

O'Herlihy, A., Worrall, A., Lelliott, P., Jaffa, T., Hill, P. and Banerjee, S. (2003). Distribution and characteristics of in-patient child and adolescent mental health services in England and Wales. *Clinical Child Psychology and Psychiatry*, *9*, 579–588.

Olmsted, M.P., Davis, R., Garner, D.M., Eagle, M., Rockert, W. and Irvine, M.J. (1991). Efficacy of a brief group psychoeducational intervention for bulimia nervosa. *Behaviour Research and Therapy*, *29*, 71–83.

Palmer, R.L., Birchall, H., McGrain, L. and Sullivan, V. (2002). Self-help for bulimic disorders: a randomised controlled trial comparing minimal guidance with face-to-face or telephone guidance. *British Journal of Psychiatry*, *181*, 230–235.

Persons, J. (1989). *Cognitive therapy in practice: a case formulation approach*. New York: Norton.

Pretorius, N., Arcelus, J., Beecham, J., Dawson, H., *et al.* (submitted). Cognitive-behavioural therapy for adolescents with bulimia nervosa: the acceptability and effectiveness of Internet-based delivery.

Prochaska, J. and DiClemente, C. (1986). Toward comprehensive model of change. In W.R. Miller and N. Heather (eds) *Treating addictive behaviors* (pp. 3–27). New York: Plenum.

Prochaska, J. and DiClemente, C. (1992). Stages of change in the modification of problem behaviours. In M. Hersen, R. Eisler and P. Miller (eds) *Progress in behaviour modification* (vol. 28, pp. 184–214). Sycamore, IL: Sycamore Publications.

Quadflieg, N. and Fichter, M. (2003). The course and outcome of bulimia nervosa. *European Child and Adolescent Psychiatry*, *12*, 99–109.

Robin, A.L., Siegel, P.T., Moye, A.W., Gilroy, M., Dennis, A.B. and Sikand, A. (1999). A controlled comparison of family versus individual therapy for adolescents with anorexia nervosa. *Journal of the American Academy of Child and Adolescent Psychiatry*, *38*, 1482–1489.

Russell, G.F.M. (1979). Bulimia nervosa: an ominous variant of anorexia nervosa. *Psychological Medicine*, *9*, 429–448.

Russell, G.F.M., Szmukler, G.I., Dare, C. and Eisler, I. (1987). An evaluation of family therapy in anorexia nervosa and bulimia nervosa. *Psychological Medicine*, *9*, 429–448.

Safer, D.L., Telch, C.F. and Agras, W.S. (2001). Dialectical behaviour therapy for bulimia nervosa. *American Journal of Eating Disorders*, *30*, 101–106.

Schmidt, U., Andiappan, M., Grover, M., Robinson, S., Perkins, S., Dugmore, O., *et al.* (2007, submitted). A randomised controlled trial of the effectiveness of a CD-ROM based cognitive behavioural self-care intervention for bulimia nervosa.

Schmidt, U., Lee, S., Beecham, J., Perkins, S., Treasure, J., Yi, I., *et al.* (2007). A randomized controlled trial of family therapy and cognitive behavior therapy guided self-care for adolescents with bulimia nervosa and related disorders. *American Journal of Psychiatry*, *164*, 591–598.

Schmidt, U. and Treasure, J. (1993). *Getting better bit(e) by bit(e). A survival kit for sufferers of bulimia nervosa and binge eating disorders*. Hove: Psychology Press.

Scholz, M. and Asen, E. (2001). Multiple family therapy with eating disordered adolescents: concepts and preliminary results. *European Eating Disorders Review*, *9*, 1, 33–42.

Shafran, R., Cooper, Z. and Fairburn, C. (2002). Clinical perfectionism: a cognitive-behavioural analysis. *Behaviour Research and Therapy*, *40*, 773–791.

Slade, P. (1982). Towards a functional analysis of anorexia nervosa and bulimia nervosa. *British Journal of Clinical Psychology*, *21*, 167–179.

Stallard, P. (2002). *Think good – feel good: a cognitive therapy workbook for children and young people*. Chichester, UK: Wiley.

Steinhausen, H.-C. (2002). The outcome of anorexia nervosa in the twentieth century. *American Journal of Psychiatry*, *159* 8, 1284–1293.

Stewart, A. (2004). Disorders of eating control. In P.J. Graham (ed.) *Cognitive behaviour therapy for children and families* (2nd edn, pp. 359–384). Cambridge: Cambridge University Press.

Stewart, J., Christner, R. and Freeman, A. (2007). An introduction to cognitive behaviour group therapy with youth. In R. Christner, J. Stewart and A. Freeman (eds) *Handbook of cognitive behaviour group therapy with children and adolescents* (pp. 3–21). New York: Routledge.

Strober, M., Freeman, R. and Morrell, W. (1997). The long-term course of severe anorexia nervosa in adolescents: survival analysis of recovery, relapse, and outcome predictors over 10–15 years in a prospective study. *International Journal of Eating Disorders*, *22*, 339–360.

Treasure, J.L. and Ward, A. (1997). A practical guide to the use of motivational interviewing in anorexia nervosa. *European Eating Disorders Review*, *5*, 102–114.

Treasure, J., Todd, G., Brolly, M., Tiller, J., Nehmed, A. and Denman, F. (1995). A pilot study of a randomised controlled trial of cognitive analytical therapy vs. educational behavioural therapy for adult anorexia nervosa. *Behaviour Research and Therapy*, *33*, 363–367.

Waller, G., Cordery, H., Corstophine, E., Hinrichsen, H., Lawson, R., Mountford, V., *et al.* (2007a). Cognitive behavioural therapy for eating disorders: a comprehensive treatment guide. Cambridge: Cambridge University Press.

Waller, G., Kennerley, H. and Ohanian, V. (2007b). Schema-focused cognitive behaviour therapy with eating disorders. In L.P. Riso, P.T. du Toit, D.J. Stein and J.E. Young (eds) *Cognitive schemas and core beliefs in psychiatric disorders: a scientist-practitioner guide* (pp. 139–175). New York: American Psychological Association.

Wells, A. (1997). *Cognitive therapy of anxiety disorders: a practice manual and conceptual guide* (pp. 80–85). Chichester, UK: Wiley.

World Health Organisation (1992). *The international classification of mental and behavioural disorders* (10th revision) (ICD-10). Geneva: WHO.

Young, J.E. (1999). *Cognitive therapy for personality disorders: a schema focused approach* (3rd edn). Sarasota, FL: Professional Resource Press.

Handout 1

BMI/target weight calculator for boys aged 11–18

Per-centile	11 Years		12 Years		13 Years		14 Years		15 Years		16 Years		17 Years		18 Years	
	25th	50th	25th	50th	25th	50th	25th	50th	25th	50th	25th	50th	25th	50th	25th	50th
BMI height in m	15.8	16.9	16.3	17.4	16.8	18	17.4	18.7	18	19.3	18.5	20	19.1	20.5	19.6	21.1
1.35	28.8	30.8	29.7	31.7	30.6	32.8	31.7	34.1	32.8	35.2	33.7	36.5	34.8	37.4	35.7	38.5
1.37	29.7	31.7	30.6	32.7	31.5	33.8	32.7	35.1	33.8	36.2	34.7	37.5	35.8	38.5	36.8	39.6
1.39	30.5	32.7	31.5	33.6	32.5	34.8	33.6	36.1	34.8	37.3	35.7	38.6	36.9	39.6	37.9	40.8
1.41	31.4	33.6	32.4	34.6	33.4	35.8	34.6	37.2	35.8	38.4	36.8	39.8	38.0	40.8	39.0	41.9
1.43	32.3	34.6	33.3	35.6	34.4	36.8	35.6	38.2	36.8	39.5	37.8	40.9	39.1	41.9	40.1	43.1
1.45	33.2	35.5	34.3	36.6	35.3	37.8	36.6	39.3	37.8	40.6	38.9	42.1	40.2	43.1	41.2	44.4
1.47	34.1	36.5	35.2	37.6	36.3	38.9	37.6	40.4	38.9	41.7	40.0	43.2	41.3	44.3	42.4	45.6
1.49	35.1	37.5	36.2	38.6	37.3	40.0	38.6	41.5	40.0	42.8	41.1	44.4	42.4	45.5	43.5	46.8
1.51	36.0	38.5	37.2	39.7	38.3	41.0	39.7	42.6	41.0	44.0	42.2	45.6	43.5	46.7	44.7	48.1
1.53	37.0	39.6	38.2	40.7	39.3	42.1	40.7	43.8	42.1	45.2	43.3	46.8	44.7	48.0	45.9	49.4
1.54	37.5	40.1	38.7	41.3	39.8	42.7	41.3	44.3	42.7	45.8	43.9	47.4	45.3	48.6	46.5	50.0
1.55	38.0	40.6	39.2	41.8	40.4	43.2	41.8	44.9	43.2	46.4	44.4	48.1	45.9	49.3	47.1	50.7
1.56	38.5	41.1	39.7	42.3	40.9	43.8	42.3	45.5	43.8	47.0	45.0	48.7	46.5	49.9	47.7	51.3
1.57	38.9	41.7	40.2	42.9	41.4	44.4	42.9	46.1	44.4	47.6	45.6	49.3	47.1	50.5	48.3	52.0
1.58	39.4	42.2	40.7	43.4	41.9	44.9	43.4	46.7	44.9	48.2	46.2	49.9	47.7	51.2	48.9	52.7
1.59	39.9	42.7	41.2	44.0	42.5	45.5	44.0	47.3	45.5	48.8	46.8	50.6	48.3	51.8	49.6	53.3
1.60	40.4	43.3	41.7	44.5	43.0	46.1	44.5	47.9	46.1	49.4	47.4	51.2	48.9	52.5	50.2	54.0
1.61	41.0	43.8	42.3	45.1	43.5	46.7	45.1	48.5	46.7	50.0	48.0	51.8	49.5	53.1	50.8	54.7
1.62	41.5	44.4	42.8	45.7	44.1	47.2	45.7	49.1	47.2	50.7	48.6	52.5	50.1	53.8	51.4	55.4

Height in m	11 Years 25th	11 Years 50th	12 Years 25th	12 Years 50th	13 Years 25th	13 Years 50th	14 Years 25th	14 Years 50th	15 Years 25th	15 Years 50th	16 Years 25th	16 Years 50th	17 Years 25th	17 Years 50th	18 Years 25th	18 Years 50th
1.63	42.0	44.9	43.3	46.2	44.6	47.8	46.2	49.7	47.8	51.3	49.2	53.1	50.7	54.5	52.1	56.1
1.64	42.5	45.5	43.8	46.8	45.2	48.4	46.8	50.3	48.4	51.9	49.8	53.8	51.4	55.1	52.7	56.8
1.65	43.0	46.0	44.4	47.4	45.7	49.0	47.4	50.9	49.0	52.5	50.4	54.5	52.0	55.8	53.4	57.4
1.66	43.5	46.6	44.9	47.9	46.3	49.6	47.9	51.5	49.6	53.2	51.0	55.1	52.6	56.5	54.0	58.1
1.67	44.1	47.1	45.5	48.5	46.9	50.2	48.5	52.2	50.2	53.8	51.6	55.8	53.3	57.2	54.7	58.8
1.68	44.6	47.7	46.0	49.1	47.4	50.8	49.1	52.8	50.8	54.5	52.2	56.4	53.9	57.9	55.3	59.6
1.69	45.1	48.3	46.6	49.7	48.0	51.4	49.7	53.4	51.4	55.1	52.8	57.1	54.6	58.6	56.0	60.3
1.70	45.7	48.8	47.1	50.3	48.6	52.0	50.3	54.0	52.0	55.8	53.5	57.8	55.2	59.2	56.6	61.0
1.71	46.2	49.4	47.7	50.9	49.1	52.6	50.9	54.7	52.6	56.4	54.1	58.5	55.9	59.9	57.3	61.7
1.72	46.7	50.0	48.2	51.5	49.7	53.3	51.5	55.3	53.3	57.1	54.7	59.2	56.5	60.6	58.0	62.4
1.73	47.3	50.6	48.8	52.1	50.3	53.9	52.1	56.0	53.9	57.8	55.4	59.9	57.2	61.4	58.7	63.2
1.74	47.8	51.2	49.3	52.7	50.9	54.5	52.7	56.6	54.5	58.4	56.0	60.6	57.8	62.1	59.3	63.9
1.75	48.4	51.8	49.9	53.3	51.5	55.1	53.3	57.3	55.1	59.1	56.7	61.3	58.5	62.8	60.0	64.6
1.76	48.9	52.3	50.5	53.9	52.0	55.8	53.9	57.9	55.8	59.8	57.3	62.0	59.2	63.5	60.7	65.4
1.77	49.5	52.9	51.1	54.5	52.6	56.4	54.5	58.6	56.4	60.5	58.0	62.7	59.8	64.2	61.4	66.1
1.78	50.1	53.5	51.6	55.1	53.2	57.0	55.1	59.2	57.0	61.2	58.6	63.4	60.5	65.0	62.1	66.9
1.79	50.6	54.1	52.2	55.8	53.8	57.7	55.8	59.9	57.7	61.8	59.3	64.1	61.2	65.7	62.8	67.6
1.80	51.2	54.8	52.8	56.4	54.4	58.3	56.4	60.6	58.3	62.5	59.9	64.8	61.9	66.4	63.5	68.4
1.81	51.8	55.4	53.4	57.0	55.0	59.0	57.0	61.3	59.0	63.2	60.6	65.5	62.6	67.2	64.2	69.1
1.82	52.3	56.0	54.0	57.6	55.6	59.6	57.6	61.9	59.6	63.9	61.3	66.2	63.3	67.9	64.9	69.9
1.84	53.5	57.2	55.2	58.9	56.9	60.9	58.9	63.3	60.9	65.3	62.6	67.7	64.7	69.4	66.4	71.4
1.86	54.7	58.5	56.4	60.2	58.1	62.3	60.2	64.7	62.3	66.8	64.0	69.2	66.1	70.9	67.8	73.0
1.88	55.8	59.7	57.6	61.5	59.4	63.6	61.5	66.1	63.6	68.2	65.4	70.7	67.5	72.5	69.3	74.6
1.90	57.0	61.0	58.8	62.8	60.6	65.0	62.8	67.5	65.0	69.7	66.8	72.2	69.0	74.0	70.8	76.2
1.92	58.2	62.3	60.1	64.1	61.9	66.4	64.1	68.9	66.4	71.1	68.2	73.7	70.4	75.6	72.3	77.8
1.94	59.5	63.6	61.3	65.5	63.2	67.7	65.5	70.4	67.7	72.6	69.6	75.3	71.9	77.2	73.8	79.4
1.96	60.7	64.9	62.6	66.8	64.5	69.1	66.8	71.8	69.1	74.1	71.1	76.8	73.4	78.8	75.3	81.1
1.98	61.9	66.3	63.9	68.2	65.9	70.6	68.2	73.3	70.6	75.7	72.5	78.4	74.9	80.4	76.8	82.7
Height	15.8	16.9	16.3	17.4	16.8	18	17.4	18.7	18	19.3	18.5	20	19.1	20.5	19.6	21.1
BMI percentile	25th	50th	25th	50th	25th	50th	25th	50th	25th	50th	25th	50th	25th	50th	25th	50th

Handout 2

BMI/target weight calculator for girls aged 11–18

Per-centile	11 Years		12 Years		13 Years		14 Years		15 Years		16 Years		17 Years		18 Years	
	25th	50th	25th	50th	25th	50th	25th	50th	25th	50th	25th	50th	25th	50th	25th	50th
BMI height in m	16.1	17.5	16.7	18.1	17.3	18.8	17.9	19.4	18.4	20.0	18.8	20.4	19.2	20.8	19.6	21.2
1.35	29.3	31.9	30.4	33.0	31.5	34.3	32.6	35.4	33.5	36.5	34.3	37.2	35.0	37.9	35.7	38.6
1.37	30.2	32.8	31.3	34.0	32.5	35.3	33.6	36.4	34.5	37.5	35.3	38.3	36.0	39.0	36.8	39.8
1.39	31.1	33.8	32.3	35.0	33.4	36.3	34.6	37.5	35.6	38.6	36.3	39.4	37.1	40.2	37.9	41.0
1.40	31.6	34.3	32.7	35.5	33.9	36.8	35.1	38.0	36.1	39.2	36.8	40.0	37.6	40.8	38.4	41.6
1.41	32.0	34.8	33.2	36.0	34.4	37.4	35.6	38.6	36.6	39.8	37.4	40.6	38.2	41.4	39.0	42.1
1.42	32.5	35.3	33.7	36.5	34.9	37.9	36.1	39.1	37.1	40.3	37.9	41.1	38.7	41.9	39.5	42.7
1.43	32.9	35.8	34.1	37.0	35.4	38.4	36.6	39.7	37.6	40.9	38.4	41.7	39.3	42.5	40.1	43.4
1.44	33.4	36.3	34.6	37.5	35.9	39.0	37.1	40.2	38.2	41.5	39.0	42.3	39.8	43.1	40.6	44.0
1.45	33.9	36.8	35.1	38.1	36.4	39.5	37.6	40.8	38.7	42.1	39.5	42.9	40.4	43.7	41.2	44.6
1.46	34.3	37.3	35.6	38.6	36.9	40.1	38.2	41.4	39.2	42.6	40.1	43.5	40.9	44.3	41.8	45.2
1.47	34.8	37.8	36.1	39.1	37.4	40.6	38.7	41.9	39.8	43.2	40.6	44.1	41.5	44.9	42.4	45.8
1.48	35.3	38.3	36.6	39.6	37.9	41.2	39.2	42.5	40.3	43.8	41.2	44.7	42.1	45.6	42.9	46.4
1.49	35.7	38.9	37.1	40.2	38.4	41.7	39.7	43.1	40.8	44.4	41.7	45.3	42.6	46.2	43.5	47.1
1.50	36.2	39.4	37.6	40.7	38.9	42.3	40.3	43.7	41.4	45.0	42.3	45.9	43.2	46.8	44.1	47.7
1.51	36.7	39.9	38.1	41.3	39.4	42.9	40.8	44.2	42.0	45.6	42.9	46.5	43.8	47.4	44.7	48.3
1.52	37.2	40.4	38.6	41.8	40.0	43.4	41.4	44.8	42.5	46.2	43.4	47.1	44.4	48.1	45.3	49.0
1.53	37.7	41.0	39.1	42.4	40.5	44.0	41.9	45.4	43.1	46.8	44.0	47.8	44.9	48.7	45.9	49.6
1.54	38.2	41.5	39.6	42.9	41.0	44.6	42.5	46.0	43.6	47.4	44.6	48.4	45.5	49.3	46.5	50.3
1.55	38.7	42.0	40.1	43.5	41.6	45.2	43.0	46.6	44.2	48.1	45.2	49.0	46.1	50.0	47.1	50.9

Height in m	11 Years		12 Years		13 Years		14 Years		15 Years		16 Years		17 Years		18 Years	
BMI percentile	25th	50th	25th	50th	25th	50th	25th	50th	25th	50th	25th	50th	25th	50th	25th	50th
1.56	39.2	42.6	40.6	44.0	42.1	45.8	43.6	47.2	44.8	48.7	45.8	49.6	46.7	50.6	47.7	51.6
1.57	39.7	43.1	41.2	44.6	42.6	46.3	44.1	47.8	45.4	49.3	46.3	50.3	47.3	51.3	48.3	52.3
1.58	40.2	43.7	41.7	45.2	43.2	46.9	44.7	48.4	45.9	49.9	46.9	50.9	47.9	51.9	48.9	52.9
1.59	40.7	44.2	42.2	45.8	43.7	47.5	45.3	49.0	46.5	50.6	47.5	51.6	48.5	52.6	49.6	53.6
1.60	41.2	44.8	42.8	46.3	44.3	48.1	45.8	49.7	47.1	51.2	48.1	52.2	49.2	53.2	50.2	54.3
1.61	41.7	45.4	43.3	46.9	44.8	48.7	46.4	50.3	47.7	51.8	48.7	52.9	49.8	53.9	50.8	55.0
1.62	42.3	45.9	43.8	47.5	45.4	49.3	47.0	50.9	48.3	52.5	49.3	53.5	50.4	54.6	51.4	55.6
1.63	42.8	46.5	44.4	48.1	46.0	49.9	47.6	51.5	48.9	53.1	49.9	54.2	51.0	55.3	52.1	56.3
1.64	43.3	47.1	44.9	48.7	46.5	50.6	48.1	52.2	49.5	53.8	50.6	54.9	51.6	55.9	52.7	57.0
1.65	43.8	47.6	45.5	49.3	47.1	51.2	48.7	52.8	50.1	54.5	51.2	55.5	52.3	56.6	53.4	57.7
1.66	44.4	48.2	46.0	49.9	47.7	51.8	49.3	53.5	50.7	55.1	51.8	56.2	52.9	57.3	54.0	58.4
1.67	44.9	48.8	46.6	50.5	48.2	52.4	49.9	54.1	51.3	55.8	52.4	56.9	53.5	58.0	54.7	59.1
1.68	45.4	49.4	47.1	51.1	48.8	53.1	50.5	54.8	51.9	56.4	53.1	57.6	54.2	58.7	55.3	59.8
1.69	46.0	50.0	47.7	51.7	49.4	53.7	51.1	55.4	52.6	57.1	53.7	58.3	54.8	59.4	56.0	60.5
1.70	46.5	50.6	48.3	52.3	50.0	54.3	51.7	56.1	53.2	57.8	54.3	59.0	55.5	60.1	56.6	61.3
1.71	47.1	51.2	48.8	52.9	50.6	55.0	52.3	56.7	53.8	58.5	55.0	59.7	56.1	60.8	57.3	62.0
1.72	47.6	51.8	49.4	53.5	51.2	55.6	53.0	57.4	54.4	59.2	55.6	60.4	56.8	61.5	58.0	62.7
1.73	48.2	52.4	50.0	54.2	51.8	56.3	53.6	58.1	55.1	59.9	56.3	61.1	57.5	62.3	58.7	63.4
1.74	48.7	53.0	50.6	54.8	52.4	56.9	54.2	58.7	55.7	60.6	56.9	61.8	58.1	63.0	59.3	64.2
1.76	49.9	54.2	51.7	56.1	53.6	58.2	55.4	60.1	57.0	62.0	58.2	63.2	59.5	64.4	60.7	65.7
1.78	51.0	55.4	52.9	57.3	54.8	59.6	56.7	61.5	58.3	63.4	59.6	64.6	60.8	65.9	62.1	67.2
1.80	52.2	56.7	54.1	58.6	56.1	60.9	58.0	62.9	59.6	64.8	60.9	66.1	62.2	67.4	63.5	68.7
1.82	53.3	58.0	55.3	60.0	57.3	62.3	59.3	64.3	60.9	66.2	62.3	67.6	63.6	68.9	64.9	70.2
Height in m / BMI percentile	16.1	17.5	16.7	18.1	17.3	18.8	17.9	19.4	18.4	20.0	18.8	20.4	19.2	20.8	19.6	21.2

Handout 3

Diary-keeping guidelines

1   Diary keeping will help you understand patterns in your behaviour and how that behaviour is influenced by your thoughts and mood, and vice versa.
2   Through diary keeping, you will learn that you can have control over your eating behaviour and that episodes of abstinence, bingeing or vomiting generally do not just 'happen' without any warning or for no reason.
3   Seeing your thoughts, feelings and behaviours in black and white can help you to be more objective about them, and that will help you to find alternative strategies.
4   While it is ultimately your diary and not the therapist's, it is important that it is brought to each session, so that the therapist has as much information as possible to use to help you recover.
5   The process of recording behaviour is in itself likely to bring about change. Diary keeping is a constant reminder of the task at hand and makes it less easy for you to turn a blind eye to your behaviour.

What diary keeping is NOT

*   A *food diary*. While you will be recording your food and fluid intake, it is not the only thing that I am interested in – information about your thoughts, feelings and behaviour generally is also very important.
*   An *exercise that you do for my benefit only*. While I will want to look at your diary with you, it is ultimately *your* diary and will help *you* to change.
*   A *test*. The diary is not intended to catch you out, and there are no right or wrong responses. I am interested in how you think, feel and behave, NOT your views on how you think you *should* be.
*   A *retrospective account of the day/week*. It is crucial that you write things down at the time that they happen, and that means you will need to have your diary with you at all times. This is because we are not very good at remembering things, particularly if we are under stress, feeling anxious or just busy.

Handout 4

Sam and Samantha

To explore the effects of starvation on physical, psychological and social development with reference to two characters 'Sam' and 'Samantha'.

- The outlines of two characters (one thin – Sam – and one healthy – Samantha) are sketched on large sheets of paper.
- The facial features, internal organs (liver, kidneys, heart, etc.) and a sample muscle are drawn separately and pasted onto the figures.
- Flag labels and Post-it notes highlight the consequences of starvation on each body system and on social functioning in Sam.
- The physical and psychosocial changes produced in recovery are attached to Samantha.
- The caricatures can be pinned on the wall for future reference.

'This exercise is best done as a fairly light-hearted group exercise, making the figures look amusing, but with important underlying messages. It is important for the therapists not to be too prescriptive about the benefits of weight gain, but permit some ambivalence to emerge in the labelling of the characters.

Sam

Samantha

Handout 5

Example of diary page

Tuesday, 5 October					
Time	Place	Food consumed	B for a binge	Compensatory behaviour (V = vomiting, etc.)	Thoughts, feelings and behaviour
Tuesday, 5 October 8.00 am	Home	Cup of black coffee			Feel tired, but determined for this to be a good day.
10.30 am	School	Diet coke			Want a bun, but going to resist.
12.30 pm	In town	Bag of chips			Feeling good; having a laugh with friends.
4.00 pm	Coming home from school	Chocolate bar and bag of crisps	B		Hungry and bored. Have got loads of homework and not confident about doing it.
6.00 pm	In bedroom	6 biscuits	B	V – tried but no success	Trying to do geography. Not too bad but worried I couldn't bring up biscuits.
7.30 pm	At home	Small portion of lasagna, banana, cup of coffee			Anxious, planned to have binge so I could bring it up to compensate for biscuits, but Mum stopped me.
9.00 pm	Watching TV	2 chocolates			Pleased now that I wasn't sick, but a bit worried. Jeans feel tight.
10.30 pm	Bedroom	Nothing			Don't know if this is progress or not. Not sure if I want Mum to help – I need to do this on my own.

Handout 6

Eating disorder assessment measures

Interviewer-based global measures for assessment and outcome
Eating Disorder Examination (EDE) (Cooper and Fairburn, 1987). A semi-structured interview, yielding subscales of restraint, weight and shape concern, and bulimia

Morgan–Russell Average Outcome Scale (MRAOS) (Morgan and Hayward, 1988). Provides a quantitative score of 0–12 and a categorical outcome measure for anorexia nervosa (good, intermediate and poor)

Self-rating questionnaires
Eating Disorder Inventory-3 (Garner, 2004). A questionnaire covering 12 domains of eating cognitions, behaviours and social functioning. Total and subscale scores can be generated, with satisfactory validity and sensitivity to change

Eating Disorders Examination Questionnaire (EDE-Q) (Fairburn and Beglin, 1994). A self-report questionnaire version of the EDE

Children's Eating Attitudes Test (ChEAT) (Maloney et al., 1988). A variation of the adult version of EAT, assessing attitudes to eating and weight

Other (non-eating disorder specific) measures used in treatment monitoring and review (see Chapter 8)

Interviewer-based global measure of outcome
Health of the Nation Outcome Scales for Children and Adolescents (HoNOSCA) (Gowers et al., 1999). A 13-item, clinician-rated measure yielding a total severity and outcome score and shown to be reliable, valid and sensitive to change

Subject self-ratings
HoNOSCA-SR (Gowers et al., 2002). The adolescent self-rated version of HoNOSCA

Family Assessment Device (FAD) (Epstein et al., 1983). A self-report questionnaire designed to evaluate family functioning based on the seven subscales of the McMaster model

Recent Mood and Feelings Questionnaire (MFQ) (Angold et al., 1995). A 42-item questionnaire to rate depression, which has good psychometric properties in clinical adolescent samples

Index